YES, YOU CAN...

Achieve Financial Independence

Yes, You Can...
Achieve Financial Independence

BY JAMES E. STOWERS
with Jack Jonathan

Deer Publishing, Inc. ◆ Kansas City, Missouri

DEER PUBLISHING, INC.
4500 Main Street, Kansas City, Missouri 64111-7709

Stowers, James E. with Jonathan, Jack.
Yes, You Can...Achieve Financial Independence
ISBN 0-9629788-0-90

Unless otherwise noted, statistical data presented in the text and
in the charts and graphs included herein has been provided by
Investors Research Corporation, Kansas City, Missouri.

This book is dedicated to all of you who
are determined to become financially independent.

Acknowledgements

Much of the credit for refining the content of this book goes to a team of editors who provided objective criticisms: Anne Davis, Mort Singer and Nancy Buckwalter began the process. Alan Doan, Amy Smith, Eric Flamholtz, Gordon Snyder, Gunnar Hughes, John Small, Myriam McCartney, Sheldon Stahl and Steve Winn added to the improvements with further insights. We also owe our thanks to our many friends and colleagues who read the various typescripts and offered excellent suggestions. We always found that each new review brought further improvement.

We are indebted to Richard Bradford, Todd Garren and Roy W. Aikman, A.S.A. for their dedication and accuracy in compiling the extensive statistical data that appears throughout.

Our grateful thanks go to Paul Coker Jr., whose imaginative illustrations have enhanced the book. Moreover, Paul's insights improved the content with his knowledge of form matching his artistry.

Book designer Rick Cusick, along with the creative staff of Kansas City's Kuhn & Wittenborn Advertising, integrated the text, charts and illustrations into a harmonious whole.

We owe special recognition to our publishing assistants Dianne Kaake and, later, Cynthia Ralls for their patient efforts.

We are also indebted to our production team for its continuous attention to detail. Pamela Stowers and Brian Drury completed the job with enthusiasm and dedication.

Finally, the lion's share of credit must go to my beloved wife, Virginia Stowers, who was always patient and supportive through countless events along the way.

Contents

> *I am determined to try to do my best*
> *at whatever I choose to do.*
>
> JAMES E. STOWERS

Part 1: About Money

We all use money, but few of us
understand its true nature.

♦ How Money Developed
♦ Precious Metals
♦ Paper Currency
♦ Banking and State Bank Notes
♦ The Birth of Today's Money System
♦ The Federal Reserve System
♦ Money in the 20th Century
♦ Money in Circulation

Money is not actually spent;
it is traded for something you want.

♦ How Can You Obtain Money?
♦ What Can You Do with Money?

*Professional investment management
    can add real value.*

- One-Time Investment of $10,000
- An Investment of $100 a Month

*Banks are willing to lend you an umbrella,
    but when it starts to rain,
    they may ask for the umbrella back.*

Part 5: Becoming Financially Independent

*It isn't so bad to be old OR poor,
    but it's a tragedy to be old AND poor.*

- Can You Live within Your Earned Income?
- Have You Built an Emergency Reserve?
- Should You Consider Borrowing?
- Do You Want to Achieve Financial Independence?
- Are You Absolutely Determined to Accomplish
    Your Financial Goals?
- What Do You Have to Do?

*You can always find extra money to set aside
    if you are determined to do so.*

- Making Better Use of Your Time
- Working Even Harder to Do a Better Job
- Getting Your Money's Worth
- Planning for Financial Windfalls
- Trying Other Ways to Find Extra Money

An unwavering determination that nothing
   was going to prevent me from accomplishing my goals...

*I am determined to try to do my best
at whatever I choose to do.*

JAMES E. STOWERS

I wrote this book because I wanted to share with you the beliefs and personal experiences that have contributed to my success. **Yes, You Can... Achieve Financial Independence** presents a different perspective on money. This book was written for people who would like to be financially independent – those who want to enjoy peace of mind in the future while being able to do what they want to do when they want to do it. Anyone, young or old, can benefit from my ideas.

Is it an accident that I became financially independent? No. My success did not come from luck, nor did it come from a family inheritance. Instead, it came as a result of:

My desire not to be controlled by circumstances;

An unwavering determination that **nothing** was going to prevent me from accomplishing my goals;

The determination to increase my knowledge through study and experience;

and

Continuous effort.

When I was young, my father did not want me to work for money; he wanted me to concentrate on my studies and music. He also urged me to play. My first experience with money as a child in grade school was putting some of my allowance in a local bank savings account. I can vividly remember my surprise, several years later, when my mother took me to the bank to close out my account. The amount I received was only slightly more than I had put in! I learned that a savings account was a money saver, not a money maker.

I learned that a savings account was a money saver, not a money maker.

I began to learn about investing when I graduated from college. I was fascinated with the opportunities it could give me to help people improve their financial positions – **and more importantly, their lives**.

In 1952, I began working for a national company representing a large mutual fund. In my desire to try to be the best, I felt I had to strive to know more than others. Fortunately, I found a mentor in George H. Wood, an officer of the management company. George helped me learn the business. When I reflect on my four decades of business experience, it's clear that few people have had more influence than George had on my life and on the way I think. Early in our relationship, George told me that he felt there were two ways to learn: study a few books by experts, or read the opinions of many people. When I assured him that I would like to know what a lot of people thought about a topic, he said he would suggest books for me to read – only if I agreed to study each one he selected.

He was a speed reader who reviewed hundreds of books, sharing with me only those he thought I should read. My experience with George was worth more than my two college degrees. In fact, I like to think that I've earned a third degree from the School of Hard Knocks. At the time I was poring over George's selections, I was making my living entirely from commissions on the investments and life insurance policies I sold –

I received no salary. When your livelihood depends entirely on sales commissions, you often learn the hard way that how you **communicate** with people means everything – a fact George hammered home. "You're not there to tell people what they **should** do," George said. "Your job is to make them aware of what they **can** do." After meeting with a prospective client, I would sit down and reconstruct our conversation in writing, to make sure I had followed George's advice.

In this book, I will share with you many of the beliefs that ultimately formed the foundation for my success in business.

As I tried to help people improve their financial positions, it became apparent that they had to protect their families with life insurance before they could even think about starting an investment program. If I had encouraged them to do otherwise, it would have been a disservice.

During that time, few life insurance companies were willing to offer the kind of policy that would give people the most protection for the least amount of money. I became convinced that low-cost, permanent annual renewable term policies represented the best value. A group of us who shared this belief decided to form a life insurance company that would offer a policy we were willing to buy ourselves. We wanted to give it a name that would best describe the type of insurance we planned

...he said he'd suggest books for me to read – only if I agreed to study each one he selected.

to offer and came up with "Death Benefit Insurance Company." It was perhaps too accurate. Our medical director suggested we put a little life into it with the name "Survivors' Benefit Insurance Company." Of course, we agreed.

The company I was working for heard of our plans and told me to either forget them or leave, so I said good-bye.

We were proud of our life insurance company. As far as we know, it was the first company to offer **pure permanent annual renewable term insurance**, renewable to age 100.

While we were starting Survivors' Benefit, I also formed a broker-dealer firm to offer nationally known mutual funds. Our sales representatives were paid high commissions for selling these funds. By the end of our first year, the representatives were earning money, but our profits were not worth our efforts. I realized that, if we were to become profitable as a company, I would have to start my own mutual fund. So, in 1958, I founded Twentieth Century Investors, Inc. offering two mutual funds with initial assets of only $100,000. At first, we employed only four people. Later, in 1980, we chose to sell the life insurance company so that we could devote all of our efforts to the success of the mutual funds. The mutual fund business grew slowly; but, by the end of 1991, over 1,000 people managed and serviced more than $15 billion in 13 different funds. Over time, we have won the confidence of more than 1,000,000 investors in our ability to manage money. In fact, our two original equity funds were ranked #1 and #3 out of all mutual funds for the 20 years ending December 31, 1991.*

Having finally succeeded after all these years, I have never lost my desire to try to be the best. I have always wanted to do my utmost to help people improve their financial positions so they can eventually become financially independent. I am still convinced that **if I help people become successful, they, in turn, will help me become successful**.

If you are determined to improve your financial position and to strive for financial independence, you need to be aware of the opportunities that are available and of the many principles and facts that can affect your future. To start with, you need to have a prepared mind. It is helpful to better understand money – its history, uses and potential. In

*Source: Lipper Analytical Services, Inc., an independent ranking service.

addition, it is important to fully comprehend the extraordinary power of compounding, the shrinking value of a dollar and the crucial importance of time in investing.

This book will lead you through the "financial forest" as painlessly as possible, with touches of humor, a sprinkling of philosophy and a heavy dose of hard facts. READ IT, DIGEST IT, APPLY IT. **This process may be one of the most important financial undertakings of your life.**

About Money

A Brief History of Money

A Brief History of Money

*We all use money, but few
of us understand its true nature.*

How Money Developed

Long ago no one needed money. Our ancestors grew their own food or hunted for it. As their skills evolved, many people realized they were better at performing some tasks, while others found satisfaction in accomplishing other chores.

In time, man's desire to acquire something he could not make or grow inspired him to start trading his particular skills or goods for services or products someone else could provide. Trading articles or services without the use of money is called "bartering." Anthropologists believe that tribes in Europe and Asia routinely met to exchange goods as early as 12,000 years ago.

Tomatoes might be valuable...but only if they were not held too long.

Bartering worked fairly well for thousands of years but it was cumbersome and often inconvenient. A farmer wanting to trade corn for a mule had to find a mule owner who wanted corn. If the mule owner wanted an axe rather than corn, the farmer was out of luck. He could search for an axe maker who would take corn and then trade for the mule, but that took time.

Value was also a problem – it constantly changed. One day an axe might be exchanged for a mule or a small cow, but not for a bushel of corn. Two weeks later, a hungry tool maker might willingly trade axes for corn. It was difficult to agree on a standard of value for making trades, and **it was not easy to save or store up value**. Tomatoes might be valuable – but only if they were not held too long.

Bars of crystal salt were used as money in many parts of Africa. Offering a bar of salt to be licked became a courtesy when one met a friend. This social custom was considered a luxury that only a few privileged people could afford.

In North America, Indians traded with "wampum" – beads made from the inner whorls of sea shells that were polished and strung together in belts. The beads were two colors, black and white; black beads were twice as valuable as white. Early settlers of New England used wampum as money when trading with the Indians for furs. In the 1700s, grain, fish, gunpowder and shot were popular forms of money.

Black beads were twice as valuable as white.

Interestingly, beer was once a form of currency. It was used as a partial payment of wages in English coal mines during the 1850s. A commission was sent to investigate beer's efficiency as money. It reported that **this "money" was popular, highly liquid, but was issued to excess, and was difficult to store**.

In all these cases, items were accepted in trade only if they were considered to have real value. But many goods had built-in drawbacks that limited their usefulness as money.

Ideally, money should be:

- ◆ Easy to handle

- ◆ Reliable, so that it may serve as a predictable and constant standard of value over time

- ◆ Universally accepted as a medium of exchange

- ◆ Divisible into easily identifiable quantities so that it can act as a more efficient unit of measurement

Precious Metals

Historians do not agree on where, when, or how precious metals were first used as money. Widely separate societies were attracted at different times by the glitter and sparkle of silver and gold. Because gold and silver were both hard to find and in great demand, someone offering precious metals could command more goods.

The Chinese used gold cubes as early as 2100 B.C., and the Bible mentions precious metals. The earliest known coins, cast in Greece around 700 B.C., were crudely inscribed gold and silver ovals. But gold and silver coins were not immune to periodic problems. For instance, Alexander the Great brought so much precious metal home from his conquests that the value of gold and silver in Greece dropped by one-third.

Paper Currency

A new form of money emerged in the Middle Ages in Europe. Because large quantities of coins were cumbersome and unsafe to transport, people taking long trips would leave their coins with goldsmiths for safekeeping and take, in return, the goldsmiths' receipt, which was worthless to a robber. At the traveler's destination, the receipt was exchanged for coins by an associate of the goldsmith. The receipts became so commonplace that people began paying debts with them rather than with coins. This marked the beginning of paper money.

The receipts became so commonplace that people began paying debts with them rather than with coins. This marked the beginning of paper money.

The use of paper money increased greatly after 1650 with the rise of national banks. For example, the Bank of Sweden, founded in 1656, printed paper bank notes which were issued to people who deposited money. These notes stated the amount of coins that a person would receive from the bank.

Years later in America, the Congress of the original 13 colonies had to finance an army during the Revolutionary War. With no taxing powers, the Congress turned to the printing presses. People were bitterly opposed to the increased amount of paper money because it lowered money's value and created higher prices for goods and services.

Banking and State Bank Notes

The United States Treasury, formed in 1789, lacked enough precious metal to issue all the coins the growing economy needed. Thus, at the local level, banks took in gold and silver deposits and made loans and payments in their own notes, which were redeemable in gold and silver. State bank notes were used widely during much of the 1800s, and by the early 1860s, more than 10,000 separate note issues of different sizes, colors and designs were in circulation. Banks had to keep a precious metal reserve on hand to meet requests for withdrawals.

...by the early 1860s more than 10,000 separate note issues of different sizes, colors and designs were in circulation.

State bank notes worked well only where people felt confident that their bank was sound and that notes could be redeemed at any time. If depositors feared a bank would not redeem their notes, they would rush to cash in their deposits for gold or silver before the reserves disappeared.

In the early 1800s, America had many honest, well-managed banks, but some earned a reputation for fraud. Even before state laws regulated banks to assure the public that the reserves were safe, vaults were built so that customers could view the precious metals. Less scrupulous bankers piled gold or silver coins on top of kegs of nails. When state examiners were sent to check reserves, some slick bank officers shipped money from bank to bank, only minutes ahead of the examiner!

The Birth of Today's Money System

The American Civil War produced changes that set the stage for today's money system. At that time, the federal government was unable to raise enough money through taxes to pay for the conflict. As rapidly as the Treasury paid bills with gold and silver coin, the metal was hoarded.

Reluctantly, Congress issued United States notes that were not redeemable in gold or silver. Congress tried to make the notes acceptable by declaring them **legal tender**, which meant that they had to be accepted in payment of all private debts.

The federal government also began chartering national banks that were given paper currency to issue. National banks received currency in proportion to the amount of government bonds they purchased. However, as the government paid off its debts after the war, the number of bonds used as backing for currency shrank. As a result, the amount of money in circulation declined, and the cash supply became inadequate to meet the needs of industry and trade. This condition led to periodic money panics until 1913 when the banking system was restructured.

The Federal Reserve System

In the early 20th century, most banks kept little cash. Small country banks deposited cash reserves at larger banks, which in turn deposited the reserves at big-city banks. This money was available to lend to businesses and brokers. This "pyramiding" of reserves hurt banks as well as the public. For instance, a bumper crop of grain would create a sudden demand for cash and cause country banks to ask for the reserves to be returned. In providing these reserves, big-city banks were left with little cash to meet the demands of their customers. Eventually, their cash ran so low that a panic started.

A severe panic in 1907 sparked the reform movement that caused Congress to create the Federal Reserve System in 1913. This system of twelve regional reserve banks was established to manage the reserves of all nationally chartered banks. The Federal Reserve Board of Governors in Washington, D.C., supervised and administered the overall operations of the system — and still does today.

The Federal Reserve lent funds to member banks so they could meet sudden and unexpected withdrawals, thus avoiding cash shortages that triggered earlier panics. Each Federal Reserve bank issued its own notes, known today as Federal Reserve Notes. These gold-backed notes were issued when each region's currency needs arose. When demand for

The Federal Reserve banks lent funds to member banks so they could meet sudden and unexpected withdrawals...

currency decreased, the notes were returned to the Federal Reserve banks as reserves for commercial banks. Thus, money was available as needed.

Money in the 20th Century

When the value of coin and paper money was tied to gold, industrial nations often had "boom" or "bust" economies. Rising gold holdings, either from new discoveries or international trade payments, increased the nation's money in circulation. If the amount of money rose faster than production output, prices soared. If gold holdings didn't keep pace with production output, prices fell and workers were laid off.

Today most money is "fiat" money, money created almost as if by magic. It is without gold backing but must be accepted as legal tender by virtue of the government's declaration.

While the use of paper money without the backing of gold and silver had been tried during the Civil War (1861-65), the modern era of **fiat money** began during the Depression in the 1930s, when most nations abandoned the rigid use of gold money and gold-backed currency. Today, most coin and currency is "fiat" money, created almost as if by magic. It is without gold backing but must be accepted as legal tender by virtue of the government's declaration. This money relies solely on the public's trust in the government. Fiat money isn't valuable in itself and does not represent a claim on gold or silver. **Money's value lies in its purchasing power**.

The story of money has been punctuated with episodes when the value of money declined dramatically. After World War I, Germany saw the worst inflation of any modern industrial country. The value of its paper money fell so low that currency was a cheaper fuel than firewood. Although economists have known for centuries that changes in the amount of money in circulation and the speed at which it is spent affects business, they didn't discover how the relationship worked until this century.

Money in Circulation

Most countries have central banks that attempt to balance the money available for spending by controlling bank reserves and bank lending – the activity that creates new money. In the United States, the Federal Reserve System is responsible for making sure that banks don't create so much money that we have inflation, or so little money that we have a recession.

The job isn't easy. No central bank has been entirely successful in maintaining the balance between too much and too little money. One problem the Federal Reserve faces is how to balance the supply of money with other major factors that affect the economy and inflation, such as government spending and taxing. Another problem is that people are unable to agree on just how much money is enough.

No central bank has been entirely successful in maintaining the balance between too much and too little money.

Just as we have gone from cows to wampum to gold, in the future the form of money transactions may change dramatically – for instance, it may take the form of "smart cards" containing a computer chip which stores the remaining dollar balance of the card after a purchase is made. Other electronic devices are now being tested which could further reduce more traditional forms of money transactions.

One problem the Federal Reserve faces is how to balance the supply of money with ... government spending and taxing.

Money is worth
only what you can
exchange for it.

Sources and Uses of Money

*Money is not actually spent;
    it is traded for something you want.*

Money is the universal medium of exchange for goods and services. It allows us to trade **value for value**, a means of trade without exchanging precious metals or bartering.

Money is worth only what you can exchange for it. In most instances, it is unlikely that you are going to exchange your money for services or goods unless you believe that the value of what you want is equal to or greater than the value you place on your cash.

How Can You Obtain Money?

Money is usually earned through wages, salaries, bonuses and commissions as a result of your effort, hard work and creativity. There is only a certain amount of money you can bring home from your personal efforts, and there is only a limited time for you to do so. Money can also come from your investments – that is, dividends, capital gains and interest. At retirement, money can come from earnings on savings, from a retirement plan and from Social Security. Money sometimes comes from gifts and inheritance or, if you are extremely lucky, from a lottery or a roll of the dice.

How can you obtain money?

What Can You Do With Money?

Money is not actually spent; it is traded for something you want. "Spending" money

Money is not actually spent; it is traded for something you want.

does not accurately describe the financial transaction. Spending implies that the dollars in the transaction disappeared, that they were used up or consumed in some way. "Trading" money more accurately describes what happens in a transaction. **Money is not consumed; it remains in circulation**.

You can do many things with money. You can:

- ◆ **Trade it**

- ◆ **Lend it**

- ◆ **Borrow it**

- ◆ **Keep it**

- ◆ **Give it away**

◆ Trading Money

Through money, you can trade the value of your services for something you want or need. If someone wants you to perform a service, you'll receive money in exchange. In this case, you are trading your time and effort for money. Later, you can trade the money you earned for goods and services you want.

The moment you trade your dollars, you no longer have them. You have something else.

The moment you trade your dollars, you no longer have them. You have something else. If you trade all of your available dollars for any one thing, you do not have that money to trade for anything else. Also, you can trade a certain sum only once. You can't trade the same money again.

Dollars can be traded for items that are consumed, such as food and clothing, or for services, such as legal assistance, health care and utilities. Money can be traded for investment ownership in items such as a home, a mutual fund or common stock. You can trade for collectibles, such as stamps, coins, art, antiques and jewelry.

◆ Lending Money

You can lend your money to individuals or institutions with the understanding that you will be paid a fixed sum of money (interest) for its use over an agreed amount of time. Then, at the end of that period, the full amount you lent will be returned to you.

Some examples of loans are:

> Savings account at a bank, savings and loan or credit union
>
> Certificates of Deposit
>
> Personal loans
>
> Government, corporate or municipal bonds

In certain transactions, you may believe you are buying something when in fact you are lending your money. For example, when you buy a Certificate of Deposit, you are making a loan to a bank.

◆ Borrowing Money

When you borrow, you pay a fixed sum (interest) regularly for use of the money over an agreed amount of time. At the end of that period, you agree to pay back the amount you originally borrowed. When you borrow money you are committing some of your future income. You are spending money you have not yet earned which has to be repaid from future earnings. If you spend the money on luxuries, you may temporarily improve your style of living, but not your financial position. On the other hand, if you borrow money to invest, i.e., "leveraging," you could improve your future financial position. Leveraging is using borrowed money to own an investment that is expected to provide higher earnings and profits than the cost of borrowing.

When you borrow money you are committing some of your future income.

Normally, the higher the risk to the lender, the higher the interest rate. When borrowing for an investment, the rate is often lower if the investment is used and accepted by the lender as collateral.

In the old days, people saved money under their mattresses...

◆ Keeping Money

If money is kept in a safe deposit box, potential income and profits are lost.

Instead of trading your money, you can keep it so that it is available to trade later for something you may want. In the old days, people saved money under their mattresses or in a cookie jar. Today you can use a safe deposit box. But, if money is kept there, potential income and profits are lost.

◆ Giving Money Away

There are many reasons for a gift of money. The act of giving generates a shared thought from the giver to the receiver. Giving money away takes many forms, such as wills, trusts or simple donations.

. . . or in a cookie jar.

The Shrinking Dollar

The Shrinking Dollar

The dollar bill has shrunk in size –
but not nearly as much as it has shrunk in value.

Compare the relative size of the 1917 bill with the size of today's
$1 bill. Today's dollar is quite a bit smaller than the older one.

(3-1)

The dollar bill has shrunk in size, but not nearly as much as it has shrunk in value.

(Illustrations of dollar bills shown at 60% of original size.)

If the **value** of today's dollar were compared with a 1900 dollar bill, you would find that its value has shrunk by 94%. Visualize the size of today's dollar shrunk by 94%. It would be about the height of the letter "e" at the end of this sentence.

The risk of **losing money** is obvious. However, the danger of money **losing value** over time is not always recognized. Sadly for many, the process by which money loses value is often understood too late, if at all.

...money is worth only what it can be exchanged for at the time of a trade.

Remember, money is worth only what it can be exchanged for at the time of a trade. The dollar has lost value when it takes more dollars to trade for items now than it did before. When you go to the store and trade $1 for bread that you previously could have bought for 50 cents, you realize your dollar has lost one-half of its value.

The following chart illustrates the decline in the value of a dollar since 1900.

(3-2)   *Decline in Value of the Dollar Since 1900*

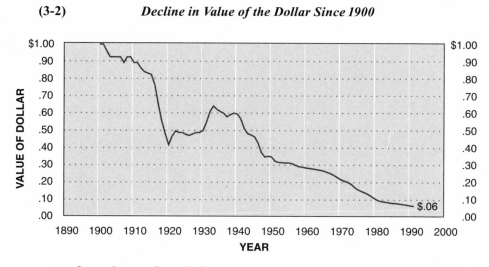

Source: Investors Research Corporation based on data provided by Bureau of the Census and Bureau of Labor Statistics.

Except for a few short periods, the dollar has continuously lost value since 1900. What happened to the value of a 1900 dollar? From 1900 through 1991, the exchange value of that dollar dropped by 94%. A dollar held since 1900 was worth only six cents on December 31, 1991. The dollar is still physically there, but its exchange value has dramatically shrunk. In fact, the value of a dollar has decreased since 1900 at the rate of slightly over 3% each year. Over the past 30 years, the value of the dollar fell at an average rate of 5% a year. For the last 20 years, the value further decreased by an average rate of 6% a year. For the past 10 years, the value fell only at a rate of 4.2% a year. However, even though the average rate of decline was slower in the last 10 years, you should be cautious in assuming that the average rate of decline will continue to lessen.

Except for a few short periods, the dollar has continuously lost value since 1900.

Learning First-Hand About the Shrinking Dollar

While I was in the service during World War II, I bought United States Government Savings Bonds to help the war effort and to save money. These bonds were purchased for $18.75. The government agreed to buy them back for $25 at maturity. Years later, I tendered these savings bonds back to the government, which lived up to its agreement and paid me $25 for each bond.

The government received $18.75 from me, kept my money for over 10 years, and then paid me $25. By that time, each dollar was worth only about 50 cents. In addition, they collected tax from me on the $6.25 interest I had earned ($25.00 - $18.75 = $6.25 interest).

I gave an $18.75 value and, 10 years later, received a $12.50 value. I was patriotic, but I learned an important financial lesson from the experience.

I gave an $18.75 value and, 10 years later, received a $12.50 value. I was patriotic, but I learned an important financial lesson from the experience.

Picture yourself as a member of Congress in Washington, D.C.... Would you have the courage to suggest that everyone's taxes be raised?

Will a Dollar Continue to Lose Value?

No one knows if the value of a dollar will continue to decline. But what has happened to a dollar in the past gives us a good indication of what may happen in the future. Consider some facts:

- ◆ Our country carries an enormous debt.

- ◆ The debt is increasing because we continue to have an unbalanced budget.

- ◆ Until the budget is balanced, the government must continue to issue new debt obligations, as it has done in the past, to finance the budget.

The financial problems of the government keep mounting. Picture yourself as a member of Congress in Washington, D.C. Now assume that you and your colleagues are faced with the problem of finding billions to help a troubled industry. How would you go about finding that money? Would you have the courage to suggest that everyone's taxes be raised? What would the people you represent think? It is apparent many elected officials fear the wrath of public opinion more than the rising national debt.

The government's need for funds **is not limited** by the requirement that money must be convertible into gold on demand. If Congress votes to expand the debt limit as it has done on many occasions, and thereby allows the Treasury to issue additional financial obligations, **the new debt will most likely serve as the source of new money in the economy**. Would many people complain? Probably not, because over the years they have become accustomed to having an unbalanced budget. For these reasons and others, the rate of loss in the value of a dollar has the potential not just to continue, but to accelerate its decline.

If a dollar loses 6.7% of its value each year for 10 years, its value will be 50 cents.

If a dollar loses 6.7% of its value each year for 10 years, its value will be 50 cents. I fear this is very likely to happen in the future, although I hope otherwise. **If it does happen however, this loss in value is probably the biggest long-term financial risk you face**. If the dollar continues to lose value every year at that rate of 6.7%, it would be worth only 12.5 cents in 30 years.

In one respect, the trouble in the United States is that the rate of loss in the value of a dollar is not occurring quickly enough! People don't realize it's happening. If the dollar lost 15% or more of its value in one year, that would certainly capture everyone's attention. Things might change in Washington.

In one respect . . .
the rate of loss in the value of the dollar is not occurring quickly enough.

Consequences of a Shrinking Dollar

To view this erosion another way: If the value of a dollar were to decrease in the future at the rate of 50% every 10 years, how might this affect you?

Everything you buy will cost twice as much. This means your income will have to double during those 10 years in order for you to maintain the same standard of living you have today. Any investments will have to double just to **stay even** – that is, multiply fourfold in 20 years, and eightfold in 30 years.

Consequences of a shrinking dollar.

For example, assume you traded $100,000 for a home today. From this time on, **your home will have its own intrinsic value. It will not be tied to the value of a dollar**. This intrinsic value will rise or fall based on the prevailing market for homes in your neighborhood but independent of the value of a dollar. In 30 years, you can trade your home back into dollars **based on the value of a dollar at that time**. If the intrinsic value of your home remained the same as it was 30 years ago, and if a dollar's value declined 6.7% each year over that time, theoretically, your home could be sold (traded) for eight times as many dollars as you paid for it – in other words, $800,000. In this example, the important concept is that your home **did not** actually appreciate in value. Rather, a dollar lost so much value that someone else would have to trade eight times as many dollars to buy it.

If your home lost some intrinsic worth during this 30-year period, because of some factor such as neglect or a deteriorating neighborhood, you might have to take less than $800,000 for it. Likewise, if the intrinsic value of your home increased during those 30 years, you might be able to trade it for more than $800,000. As you can see, a combination of factors determines the final value. **Two different "values" are involved in this example: one, the real value of the home, and two, the value of a dollar at a given time**.

What direct effect has the continuous loss in the value of a dollar had on people? In the "good old days," in 1834, you could have paid for a dinner for four in one of New York's prime restaurants, left a generous tip, and received change – all from a single dollar bill.

(3-3)

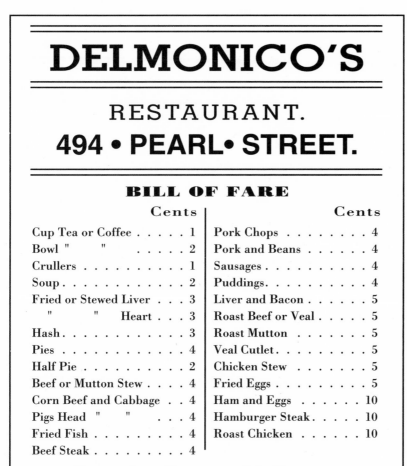

DELMONICO'S

RESTAURANT.
494 • PEARL• STREET.

BILL OF FARE

	Cents		Cents
Cup Tea or Coffee	1	Pork Chops	4
Bowl " "	2	Pork and Beans	4
Crullers	1	Sausages	4
Soup	2	Puddings.	4
Fried or Stewed Liver	3	Liver and Bacon	5
" " Heart	3	Roast Beef or Veal	5
Hash	3	Roast Mutton	5
Pies	4	Veal Cutlet.	5
Half Pie	2	Chicken Stew	5
Beef or Mutton Stew	4	Fried Eggs	5
Corn Beef and Cabbage	4	Ham and Eggs	10
Pigs Head " "	4	Hamburger Steak.	10
Fried Fish	4	Roast Chicken	10
Beef Steak	4		

Regular Dinner 12 Cents.

Do you think that the 1834 menu is too extreme an example? If so, ask your parents or people their age what it was like years ago. Ask them:

THEN	NOW
How much did they pay for their first home?	What do they think it would be worth today?
What did their first new car cost?	How much would a similar car cost now?
How much did four years of college cost?	What is the cost of a college education today?
How much did they pay for a loaf of bread?	How much does a loaf of bread cost today?

The cost of a loaf of bread, then and now, illustrates the loss in value of your money. How much does a loaf of bread cost today?

I can remember in the 1940s when 10 cents bought a loaf of bread. The other day I paid $1.35.

At this point, you can see how **people who kept their money in a "safe" place** (like the mattress or a cookie jar), thinking they were doing the right thing, **were losing real value year after year**.

One way to avoid the loss in the value of your money is to trade it quickly. Obviously, however, this move leaves you with no money in reserve for the future.

Another approach is to trade your money for something **not tied to a dollar**, something that has an opportunity to appreciate faster than the inevitable decline in the value of a dollar.

When dollars are accumulated or conserved for short periods (a few years) before being spent, the erosion in value of a dollar is limited. However, when dollars are accumulated or held for extended periods (10 to 20 years or more), such as for retirement, then the reality of money losing substantial value over time has potentially devastating consequences that must be taken into account in your investment planning.

If the Indians had invested those
$24 they were paid for Manhattan
Island at 7%, today they could buy
it back and have money left over.

The Extraordinary Power of Compounding

*"Time is money," and money is not nearly
    as valuable without time.*

The Dutch bought Manhattan Island from the Indians in 1626 – over 365 years ago – and they allegedly paid $24 for it. Were the Indians taken advantage of? If they had invested those $24 at 5% for 365 years, the investment would be worth $1.3 billion. That's assuming no taxes, of course.

(4-1)   ***$24 Invested for 365 Years (No Taxes)
            at Various Rates of Return***

(Compounded Annually)

5%	$ 1,301,000,000
6%	41,386,000,000
7%	1,274,354,000,000
8%	38,008,610,000,000
9%	1,098,709,000,000,000
10%	30,799,330,000,000,000

Nature Is a Wonderful Teacher

Look at the amazing results of planting a single seed of wheat. One seed, when planted and nurtured, can produce more than 100 seeds. **If all of these seeds were not consumed but planted** with equal tender loving care, they would produce at least 10,000 more seeds of wheat. Nature is a wonderful teacher. She can help us understand what can happen when money is allowed to compound over time.

The Importance of Time and Money

Solomon said, **"In all of your getting, get understanding."** In few areas is there less understanding than in the subject of money. Most people find it difficult to comprehend precisely what money is. For example, is $100,000 a large sum of money or a small amount? Before you jump to a conclusion, let's find out what this sum is really worth to you in your everyday life.

If you were paid your salary once in your lifetime, it might well amount to over $1,000,000. But that would be just a figure on paper until converted into a lifetime of rent or mortgage payments, groceries, clothing and utility bills.

Most people find it difficult to comprehend precisely what money is.

You know better than anyone what your paycheck represents to you. When you think of your income in terms of how much it will buy each month, you begin to understand the real value of money. To understand how much $100,000 is really worth, consider that sum as a monthly dollar amount (ignoring taxes).

If you put $100,000 in a safe place and decided to TAKE OUT equal monthly amounts for 35 years, you would be able to TAKE OUT $238 each month. After 35 years, you would have nothing left. Now, if you **invested** your $100,000 and received a 6% rate of return, Table 4-2 shows that you would receive $487 income a month FOREVER on $100,000 without invading your principal. In summary, if you had invested your money for 35 years, you could have received a total of $204,540 ($487 x 12 months x 35 years = $204,540) and **still** have your original $100,000.

When you think of your income in terms of how much it will buy each month, you begin to understand the real value of money.

The monthly amount you received could have been increased by adding a portion of your principal to the earned income, thus using all

(4-2)

The Amount You Can Receive Monthly From a $100,000 Investment

(Compounded Annually)

(%)	If You Receive Both Income and Part of the Principal				OR	If You Receive Income Only Keeping Principal FOREVER
0	$1,667	$556	$333	$238		$0
4	1,838	736	524	439		327
6	1,926	835	635	560		487
8	2,014	940	753	690		643
10	2,104	1,048	879	827		797
12	2,194	1,161	1,008	967		949
14	2,284	1,277	1,141	1,109		1,098
16	2,376	1,395	1,276	1,251		1,245
Years	5	15	25	35		

of your principal within a certain period of time. For example, if you had received a 6% rate of return on your money and you wanted nothing left after 35 years, the table above shows that you could have received $560 each month for that period. If, on the other hand, you wanted to use all of your money sooner, you could have received $835 a month for 15 years at a 6% rate of return.

If you were paid your salary once in your lifetime, it might well amount to over $1,000,000 ...

(4-3)

How Much Cash Does It Take Monthly to Provide What You Want?
(Compounded Annually)

AGE AT START — PUT IN MONTHLY to age 65

(%)	20	30	40	50	60
0	$185.19	$238.10	$333.33	$555.56	$1,667
4	67.62	111.12	196.52	408.74	1,511
6	38.13	72.80	147.87	348.54	1,439
8	20.81	46.67	110.01	296.20	1,371
10	11.09	29.42	81.08	250.98	1,306
12	5.82	18.32	59.30	212.11	1,245
14	3.03	11.31	43.12	178.87	1,186
16	1.57	6.94	31.21	150.57	1,131
YEARS	45	35	25	15	5

AGE 65

AGE ENDING — TAKE OUT MONTHLY from age 65

70	80	90	100	FOREVER	(%)
$1,667	$556	$333	$238	$0	0
1,838	736	524	439	327	4
1,926	835	635	560	487	6
2,014	940	753	690	643	8
2,104	1,048	879	827	797	10
2,194	1,161	1,008	967	949	12
2,284	1,277	1,141	1,109	1,098	14
2,376	1,395	1,276	1,251	1,245	16
5	15	25	35		YEARS

How Much Cash Does It Take Monthly to Provide a Monthly Income Later?

Table 4-3 underscores the importance of time and compounding. The figures in the left square represent the amount of money necessary to **PUT IN** each month from a given age to age 65. The figures to the right are the monthly **TAKE OUT** figures beginning at age 65. The **TAKE OUT** figures are shown for various time periods and at various compound rates of return. They represent the amount of money that can be paid to you each month from both income and principal in order to deplete all of the money by the end of a stated number of years.

The boxed column at the extreme right represents the amount of money that you can **TAKE OUT** each month at various rates of return **FOREVER** and at the same time preserve the principal sum.

This table highlights one of the most important concepts in this entire book – the power of compounding over time. Let's consider some examples to better understand the message you can derive from it. The time you take reading and re-reading to understand the principles in this chapter can pay big dividends when you are older.

If you are 20 years old and your money can earn only a 6% rate of return, you can **PUT IN** $38.13 each month from age 20 to age 65 – for 45 years. Beginning at age 65, you can **TAKE OUT** $560 each month for the next 35 years or until you reach age 100. Over the 45 years, you would **PUT IN** a total of $20,590 and you can **TAKE OUT** $235,200 from age 65 to 100 at $560 a month.

If you are more interested in spending money than in saving it, and you delay investing until age 40 to accomplish the same goal, you would have to set aside an additional $109.74 a month for the next 25 years. You would have to **PUT IN** $147.87 each month – not $38.13 a month. During the 25 years up to age 65, you would **PUT IN** a total of $44,361 in order to receive the same $235,200 from age 65

If you are more interested in spending money than in saving it, you may soon regret not paying closer attention to your financial future.

to 100. So you see, if you delayed 20 years, it would be necessary for you to PUT IN an additional $23,771 (or twice as much) in order to have the same amount you could have had by starting at age 20.

If you delayed investing until age 50 (30 years later), you would have to PUT IN $348.54 a month at 6% in order to TAKE OUT, at age 65, $560 a month until you reached 100. Over the 15-year period, you would PUT IN a total of $62,737 (over three times as much), and you would TAKE OUT $235,200 by the time you reached 100.

Remember: It is essential to start saving regularly early in life!

Time Is Truly Money

Time, as you can see from this review, is a vital factor in any serious discussion of money. The table below further underscores this point.

(4-4)   *TIME is a Vital Factor*
Using **6** percent compounded annually:

If you PUT IN	You could TAKE OUT
$ 1.00 a month for 45 years	*$14.69 a month for 35 years
$ 1.00 a month for 35 years	$ 7.69 a month for 35 years
$ 1.00 a month for 25 years	$ 3.79 a month for 35 years
$ 1.00 a month for 15 years	$ 1.61 a month for 35 years
$ 1.00 a month for 5 years	$ .39 a month for 35 years

*From Table 4-3, $560 ÷ $38.13 = $14.69

What Happens If You Can Earn Just 2% More?

Table 4-3 shows what could happen if your money earned 8% instead of 6%. If you PUT IN $20.81 a month from age 20 to age 65, you could TAKE OUT $690 a month to age 100. In this example, you would PUT IN a total of $11,237 over the 45 years. By taking out $690 a month to age 100, you would TAKE OUT a total of $289,800. The difference between these two figures ($289,800 - $11,237 = $278,563) again illustrates the power of compounding over time.

There are two major benefits of reaching for an 8% rate of return instead of 6%. The first benefit is that you PUT IN $9,353 **less** over 45 years. The second benefit is that you TAKE OUT $54,600 **more** over 35 years. The total increased benefit of reaching **2% more** here would amount to $63,953…**the magic of compounding** at work.

	6%	vs.	8%	Advantage of greater return over time
PUT IN over 45 years	$ 20,590		$ 11,237	$ 9,353
TAKE OUT over 35 years	$235,200		$289,800	$54,600
Total Advantage				$63,953

Both the **importance of time and the advantage of an increased annual rate of return** are again stressed when you compare the table below to Table 4-4.

(4-5)   *The Importance of TIME*
Using **8** percent compounded annually:

If you PUT IN	You could TAKE OUT
$ 1.00 a month for 45 years	*$33.16 a month for 35 years
$ 1.00 a month for 35 years	$14.78 a month for 35 years
$ 1.00 a month for 25 years	$ 6.27 a month for 35 years
$ 1.00 a month for 15 years	$ 2.33 a month for 35 years
$ 1.00 a month for 5 years	$ 0.50 a month for 35 years

*From Table 4-3, $690 ÷ $20.81 = $33.16

… seeking higher returns generally increases the risk.

In summary, the two critical factors in the magic of compounding are (1) **the average annual rate of return** and (2) **time**. Of these two, the most fundamental is **time**. Deferring the decision to save is costly. Every year you delay saving, makes the goal of financial independence **much more difficult**.

The higher the rate of return you can achieve, the less money you must set aside each month to accomplish your goal. However, seeking higher returns generally increases the risk. If you started at age 30, Table 4-3 indicates that at 6%, you would need to set aside $72.80 each month to age 65 to receive $560 each month to age 100. Now, if you could instead earn a rate of 8% on your money (only 2% more), and you wanted to receive the same $560 each month to age 100, it is **not** necessary for you to set aside $46.67 a month as shown in Table 4-3, (which would enable you to receive $690 a month), but rather $37.88; i.e., ($46.67 ÷ $690) x $560 = $37.88. In other words, by reaching for 8%, the amount of money that you would need to **PUT IN** to accomplish your goal ($560) would be greatly reduced (from $72.80 to $37.88). Thus, a one-third increase in the rate of return reduced the required monthly amount by nearly one-half.

How Much CASH Does It Take NOW in One Lump Sum to Provide a Monthly Income LATER?

The higher the rate of return you can achieve, the less money you must set aside each month to accomplish your goal.

In comparison, instead of setting aside money each month, how much money would you have to set aside in a single lump sum earning 6% to accomplish the same goal of receiving $560 each month from age 65 to age 100? The shaded portion of Table 4-6 indicates the amount of money necessary at various ages to illustrate this point.

(4-6)

One Lump Sum
How Much Cash Does It Take Now to Provide What You Want?
(Compounded Annually)

(%)	AGE AT START							AGE 65	AGE ENDING				KEEPING PRINCIPAL FOREVER	(%)
	Birth	10	20	30	40	50	60		70	80	90	100		
0	$100,000.00	$100,000.00	$100,000	$100,000	$100,000	$100,000	$100,000		$1,667	$556	$333	$238	$0	0
4	7,813.27	11,565.55	17,120	25,342	37,512	55,526	82,193		1,838	736	524	439	327	4
6	2,265.26	4,056.74	7,265	13,011	23,300	41,727	74,726		1,926	835	635	560	487	6
8	672.13	1,451.09	3,133	6,763	14,602	31,524	68,058		2,014	940	753	690	643	8
10	203.93	528.94	1,372	3,588	9,230	23,939	62,092		2,104	1,048	879	827	797	10
12	63.22	196.34	610	1,894	5,882	18,270	56,743		2,194	1,161	1,008	967	949	12
14	20.01	74.17	275	1,019	3,779	14,010	51,937		2,284	1,277	1,141	1,109	1,098	14
16	6.46	28.50	126	555	2,447	10,793	47,611		2,376	1,395	1,276	1,251	1,245	16
YEARS	65	55	45	35	25	15	5		5	15	25	35		
	PUT IN AT ONE TIME to age 65								TAKE OUT MONTHLY from age 65					

At age 30, it would take a one-time investment of $13,011 to accomplish your goal, using 6% compounded annually. That is, the $13,011 would be left to compound at 6% a year for 35 years in order for you to TAKE OUT $560 each month from age 65 until you reached 100. In other words, at age 30 you would have PUT IN $13,011 at one time to TAKE OUT $235,200 between age 65 and 100.

If you waited only 10 years, to age 40, it would take $23,300 (or $10,289 more) to accomplish the same financial goal of receiving $560 each month.

If, on the other hand, you reached for a higher percentage rate (8% at age 30) you would find that $6,763 would give you $690 a month from age 65 to age 100. If you wanted to receive only $560 a month, the amount needed at age 30 at 8% is not $6,763 but only $5,489; i.e., ($6,763 ÷ $690) x $560 = $5,489. By realizing an 8% average annual rate of return instead of 6%, it would take only $5,489 instead of $13,011 (42% less).

Amazing Results Over Time

Obviously, the earlier you start, the less money it takes.

It is interesting to observe that at age 20, IF you could obtain a 10% annual rate of return on your money and IF you PUT IN AT ONE TIME $1,372 and allowed it to compound until age 65 (45 years), you could TAKE OUT $827 each month or a total of $347,340 from age 65 to age 100. Subtracting the amount you PUT IN from the amount you could TAKE OUT, shows that the total amount of income you would receive would be $345,968 over and above what you invested.

The tables in this chapter illustrate the importance of reaching for the **highest average annual rate of return** you believe you can comfortably and securely receive on your investment. The higher the rate, the less money it takes to provide what you want, but the risk is higher too. **The**

importance of time is stressed in these tables. Obviously, the earlier you start, the less money it takes.

These tables are mathematical compound interest computations, and do not refer to any particular type of investment. Furthermore, they do not take taxes into consideration. They are shown to give you an idea of how much money it would take at various average annual rates of return and over various periods of time to accomplish your financial goals. They also show dramatically the power of compounding and the tremendous importance of what we all have so little of...TIME. They indicate how important it is for you to **utilize time to your best advantage**.

The Four Keys to Accumulating Wealth

In conclusion, the following points should be quite clear:

1. **Start investing as early as possible. It takes significantly less money to accomplish what you want, and you have more time working for you.**

2. **Be determined to save on a regular basis. It is an easy way to accumulate wealth.**

3. **Begin investing with the largest possible sum you can. You will have more money working for you over a longer period of time.**

4. **Reach for the highest rate of return you believe you can safely receive on your money over time. Each additional percent is important. The higher the rate, the less money it takes to accomplish what you want.**

If you would like to study additional tables about the compounding of money, turn to Addendum A.

Confronting Your Financial Challenges

What Do You Want in the Future?

What Do You Want in the Future?

Salud, pesetas, y amor, y tiempo para gozarlos.

"Health, wealth and love – and time to enjoy them" is an ancient Spanish proverb that best describes the idea that money has no value unless one has the time and good health to enjoy it.

Consider:

If you **have to be poor**, would you rather be poor **now** or **at retirement**?

Do you feel confident that **someone else** is going to take care of you if you have a financial problem?

Do you want to try to control your own destiny rather than be controlled by circumstances?

Can you commit yourself to putting order into your life so that you can accomplish your goals?

You can become financially independent – **if** you have enough time remaining and **if** you have the determination to achieve your goal.

Your purpose in life is not to save; it is to be able to do what you want to do. Unfortunately, you can't have everything. You must decide what you want the most and then make plans to acquire it. The most important step is to set priorities and then search for the means by which you can achieve your goals.

You can determine the course of your life. Financial independence is one of the means by which you can do what you want to do when you want to do it.

As you travel through life in pursuit of financial independence, you may feel it is a long journey full of obstacles. However, after you travel

...after you travel life's road and look back, that same path looks very short.

life's road and look back, that same path looks very short. You will wonder how the time could have passed so quickly.

What Challenges Do You Face?

Consider where you are today, then step back and look at some of the challenges you will face in the future:

Making a living
Keeping your job
Saving enough/not spending too much
Deciding where savings should be invested
Getting your money's worth
Providing for education
Maintaining your health
Providing for a catastrophe (emergency reserve)
Staying out of debt
Keeping up with the Joneses
Providing for child and parent care
Living too long
Dying too soon

If you are young, you may want to live a full life in a hurry. You have to have a car just as soon as you get your first job; you don't believe you can do without it. Even when just starting out, you may desire a home of your own. Probably you want all the trappings of the good life before you have really established yourself. Indeed, many of us are ready for retirement with the sound of the opening gun.

Indeed, many of us are ready for retirement with the sound of the opening gun.

Delaying what you want **now** in order to achieve financial independence in the future may not seem like much fun. Being thrifty may be something foreign to you. If your guiding principle is to satisfy as many wants as possible in the shortest time, you may not wish to put off until tomorrow what you can get on credit today. Sometimes your only restraints are those imposed by your finance company or bank.

For many of us, life unfolds this way: As we get older and our income increases, we may have extra money to spend, allowing us to reach a little higher standard of living. We move from our first home to a better one and surround ourselves with luxuries that reflect an

Sometimes your only restraints are those imposed by your finance company or bank.

...face the financial
realities of life.

increased income. We are not overly concerned about the future. We are confident that when the time comes, we will make sufficient money to provide what we want. The possibility that we might become physically unable to work or might have business reversals does not seem to dampen our optimism or curb our spending. As we move along in our careers, we see misfortunes happening to others, but we believe they won't happen to us.

This pattern can continue through our working years unless we are brought down to earth by circumstances to face the financial realities of life.

Special Challenges to Consider:

- ◆ **Getting Ahead**
- ◆ **Deciding on Your Most Important Wants**
- ◆ **Living Within Your Means**
- ◆ **Becoming Aware of Money Management**

◆ **Getting Ahead**

To earn money, most of us learn certain skills and apply them to a job. We try to be successful by learning and becoming more proficient. It takes a great deal of time, thinking, planning, determination and study to develop additional skills. But having a set of skills is not enough. We must apply them.

Financial success is seldom an accident. Prosperity almost always comes from hard work and saving over time. If you want to succeed financially, **wishing cannot replace working**. You must be determined to accomplish your goal.

◆ Deciding on Your Most Important Wants

As you earn money, you face another financial challenge. How should you use it?

Few people have unlimited resources. You bring home a certain amount and no more. This is all the money you have to work with each month. After federal, state, local and Social Security taxes, there is only a certain amount left for all of your wants. Most of us have more wants than we have income to provide them. This creates the challenge of deciding which want has priority. As soon as you realize that there isn't enough money to have everything you would like, begin to prioritize your wants. You may learn that **if you spend all of your money for a particular want, none will be left for the others**. You may also learn, perhaps the hard way, that if you spend more money than you earn, you will run out of money.

Most of us have more wants than we have income to provide them. This creates the challenge of deciding which want has priority.

Since **money can be spent (traded) only once**, you need to decide which wants are the most important. To do this, it may be helpful to place a personal value on each of your wants and rank them in order of priority. Some items on your list might be:

WANTS	VALUE TO YOU
Fancy home	Satisfying a dream
Jacuzzi	Feeling good
Stereo and video system	Entertainment
Designer clothes	Being stylish
Sports car	Fulfilling a childhood desire
Vacation home	Relaxing
Boat	Sailing, fishing
Country club	Socializing, sports and prestige
Video camera	Recording experiences
Air conditioning	Being comfortable
Swimming pool	Exercising, pleasure and status
Education for children	Providing them with a good start in life
Saving and investing	Achieving financial independence

Once you decide how to spend your income, you must also make sure you get your money's worth. **This is a real challenge**. Should you buy a cheaply-made item and possibly be forced to replace it, or should you pay more for a quality item that will last? In the long run, which is the best trade for your money?

◆ Living Within Your Means

You can easily over-extend yourself using credit. You can raise your current standard of living to such a high level that it cannot be sustained. For example, if you buy a big home, a car, furniture and major appliances on credit, you obligate yourself to making large monthly payments for many months into the future. You are committing yourself today to the way you will spend your future income. If your monthly payments and your current living expenses are greater than your income, you are in serious financial difficulty.

Forgetting You Have Money Saved

You may need to make a conscious effort to forget you have money saved. Each time you remember you have money, you may think of a way to spend it. In order to save money, you must fight to keep from spending it.

Believing You Can Run Out of Money

In order to save money, you must fight to keep from spending it.

As you age, the scales tend to shift sides. Instead of having the desire to spend money, you want to save. **You face a new challenge – the fear of running out of money**. You may be afraid that if you die too soon, your family could run out of money. Likewise, if you live too long and are unable to work, **you** may run out of money.

How much money will it take to
provide what you really want?

◆ Becoming Aware of Money Management

You may not fully understand money and how to manage it effectively, even though you **are aware** of the fundamental concepts of the importance of time and of the eroding value of a dollar.

You may not know:
How much money it will take to provide what you really want.
How much money you will need each month **for the rest of your life.**
How much money you may need for care **if you become disabled.**
How much money it will take in one lump sum to provide what you want your survivors to have **if you die.**

You may be unaware:
That what you are doing may not accomplish your financial goals.
That **managing money** is just as important as earning it.
That you could be paying too much for life insurance, or that you could be under-insured.

Why might you be unaware? You simply may not take enough time to collect the facts or to think them through; you may be too busy. You have no time to stop and think about your future, because all of your time is spent worrying about the challenges of surviving day to day.

There is another reason. You might be an expert in your own profession, but no one can be an **expert at everything**. Perhaps all of your time is spent trying to be successful in your profession; therefore, you may not have the extra time to become an expert in financial matters as well. You may not realize that managing money is just as important as earning it.

You may not realize that managing money is just as important as earning it.

We have covered some of the financial challenges you might face in the future. Taken as a whole, it may appear that you are up against an impossible task. The solution to big problems is like a statue buried in a large block of stone. The shape of the solution lies somewhere inside the stone. By chipping at it a little piece at a time, with great patience and care, you will eventually uncover the final image.

The problem solver is you. **YOU have many assets and, hopefully, good health working for you.** You also have the ability to learn, and the strength to continue to earn.

You will never have more time remaining than you have RIGHT NOW.

The time you have remaining in your life is also a precious asset. You will never have more time remaining than you have RIGHT NOW.

Take a Personal Inventory

Which of these personal assets do you have?

Physical:
    Appearance
    Energy
    Health
    Time remaining

Mental:
    Intelligence
    Creativity
    Ability to adapt and to learn

Emotional:
    Enthusiasm
    Determination
    Self-esteem
    Positive attitude
    Confidence

Professional:
 Education
 Experience
 Knowledge
 Skills and talents

Social:
 Friends and associates
 Family

Understanding and using your unique characteristics to your advantage will help you greatly in determining your financial future. Your awareness of your strengths and weaknesses will motivate you to make improvements over time.

Understanding and using your unique characteristics to your advantage will help you greatly in determining your financial future.

One of the most important assets, besides your continued good health and your time remaining, will be your determination – a persistent desire to constantly improve yourself which is one of the most important steps in becoming financially independent.

Taking a personal inventory

Planning for Daily Wants

Planning for Daily Wants

*If you spend more than you make,
    you are spending your future income.*

Planning to Live Within Your Income

It takes more than love, food, clothing and shelter to have a satisfactory life. Transportation, education, health care and entertainment help to make life more complete.

It takes more than love, food, clothing and shelter to have a satisfactory life.

Your tastes and priorities determine the number and costs of your wants. As long as the total cost of the items you purchase is less than the income you bring home, you are "living within your income." The more money you save before paying for your wants, the better prepared you will be to face future financial storms and the more money you will have to invest in your financial independence. In order not to spend more than you make, you must plan and be disciplined and determined.

If you spend more than you make, you are spending your future income. You are committing money you haven't yet earned. You are taking on a future obligation. If these commitments are monthly installment payments, you are obligating yourself to earn even more money in the future so that you can repay what you have already spent. If you spend more than you earn, you must use borrowed money to do it. Unfortunately, our society and, specifically, financial institutions encourage the use of credit – in other words, borrowing.

The Credit Card Trap

The use of charge accounts became popular years ago as a convenient way to pay for purchases made during a month. Over time, the businesses that offered charge accounts found that many people spent more than they

The Credit Card Trap

realized and were unable to pay the full balance of what they owed at the end of the month. At first, some businesses reacted by cancelling the accounts. Others, however, took advantage of the situation and turned the unpaid balances into loans, charging high interest rates to compensate for the higher risk and the lack of collateral. As a consequence, financial institutions began issuing credit cards. Some people consider charge accounts and credit cards a convenience, but for many their use is a dangerous financial trap. Adopting a policy of **cash only** can prevent you from falling into such a trap.

What if you have already fallen into the credit card trap? Frankly, your best move would be to work your unpaid balance down to zero as fast as you can. Then make a solemn vow never to fall into that trap again.

Two Basic Reasons to Borrow Money

Borrowing to invest – If we didn't borrow money to buy a home, most of us would not be able to own one. A home provides a place to live that is also an investment because it offers the potential for growth in value.

Borrowing to consume – Although many people think a new car is an investment, this is generally not true because it loses value too rapidly. In reality, if you borrow money to buy a car you are actually borrowing to consume. In our country, a car is almost a necessity. There is nothing wrong with buying a car, but why not buy one for which you can afford to pay cash?

Simply possessing or using certain things may require you to commit future dollars.

Hidden Obligations

Simply possessing or using certain things may require you to commit future dollars. For example, if you trade money for a camera, you commit future cash for film and processing costs. When you trade money to purchase a car, you commit yourself to paying for taxes, insurance, gasoline, parking and repairs. In addition, you lose the earnings on the assets tied up in your car while its value decreases with age. Similarly, when you trade money for a home, you commit to making monthly payments and to paying taxes and insurance premiums. You also trade dollars for furnishings, light, heat, cooling and maintenance. **That is, you have committed the use of part of your future earnings. In other words, it often costs more than the purchase price to own something**.

Having Second Thoughts

Before we were married, my future wife, Virginia, who was just out of nursing school wanted to buy a car. She received money from her father for a car and asked me to help her find a good used one. I asked her whether she would be able to afford all the other expenses that went with owning a car if she bought one. After thinking about it, she deferred the purchase, returned the money to her father, and found she was able to manage by walking and riding the bus.

Before buying your next car, consider the options. Do you want to live within your income, prioritize your wants and pay cash for transportation? Or do you want to borrow money to buy a car and obligate your future earnings?

The point of this example is that **if you want to achieve financial independence, you must plan and be disciplined and determined to control your wants**. You don't want to find yourself buying things that cost more than you expect (due to their upkeep) or **mortgaging your future** by spending more than you make, especially if you cannot afford the extra expense.

If you don't have enough money to buy what you want, why borrow money to buy it now?

If you don't have enough money to buy what you want, why borrow money to buy it now? Why not wait until you can afford it? Why not make up your mind that you will never borrow money for anything you intend to consume, such as food, clothing and transportation? Can you live within your income? The answer is "yes" if you decide not to buy until you have the money.

Planning for Emergencies

Planning for Emergencies

If you don't provide for your emergencies, who will?

Life is full of risks and financial pitfalls. As an income earner, you must consider the unpleasant possibility that something may happen to affect your earning ability and therefore impact your current lifestyle and deter you from achieving your financial goals. In some respects, the world in which we live can be hazardous to our financial health. In planning our future, we must take into account the consequences of these risks.

The world in which we live can be hazardous to our financial health.

For the sake of simplicity, these risks can be divided into three categories: Personal, Property and Business.

Personal Risks

Health	Accident
Short-term disability	Temporary disability
Long-term disability	Permanent disability

Property Risks
 Fire
 Accidents
  Home
  Car
  Robbery
 Nature
  Earthquake
  Hurricane
  Storms (tornado,
  lightning, flood, etc.)

Business Risks
 Termination
 Business failure
 Strike

There also might be risks unique to your special occupation.

The probability of you facing the consequences of many of these risks is remote, and the likelihood of a number of them happening in a short period is extremely remote. **But any one of them could happen to you.**

Should any of these events occur, however, a considerable amount of money might be required to meet expenses. There also might be other risks unique to your special occupation. If something **does** happen, you should be prepared to cope with it. Do you want to be in control, or are you willing to be at the mercy of unforeseen events?

Your Emergency Reserve

Your first priority should be to build an emergency reserve. You would be wise to set aside between three and six months of living expenses in easily accessible savings. If you are not working or if you are planning to retire, you may wish to transfer some of your long-term assets to your emergency reserve, increasing it to six months or more. The amount of your emergency reserve may vary according to the flexibility of your budget and your comfort zone. Bear in mind that these liquid assets are there to see you through financial storms while you maintain a long-term strategy to protect the value of other investments.

Your emergency reserve is not intended to cover all possible risks. For complete protection, including such things as long-term disability and fire protection, you clearly need to have insurance.

When purchasing insurance, you can normally save a considerable amount on premiums by **using high deductibles**, which you can pay out of the emergency reserve if the need arises.

After you have decided the amount you want in your emergency reserve, consider where this reserve will be kept. Your reserve should be:

> **Readily available** on short notice (liquid)
>
> **Safe**, with the return of your money assured
>
> **Income-producing**

Several options that meet all these criteria are:

> Banks
>
> Credit unions
>
> Savings and loans
>
> Money market mutual funds

Your choice of investment instruments should depend on their ease of access and how much safety they offer you.

…liquid assets are there to see you through financial storms.

Planning for Your Survivors

My INTENT *in this section is to convey several fundamental messages for anyone who wishes to provide for a loved one. While there are many family lifestyles, this section takes a "case study" approach, assuming that you are a husband who wishes to provide for your wife, a research scientist who does not have much experience in managing money. Recognizing the growing participation of women in business and as providers, the ideas and examples in the next three chapters (8, 9 and 10) can apply to anyone, male or female.*

How Much Money Is Needed?

How Much Money Is Needed?

*We all face the reality that we will die someday;
the only question is "when?"*

You are confident that, in one way or another, while you live you will be able to provide for yourself and your loved ones. However, what happens if you do not live? No one knows what the future has in store. You should consider all the possibilities when planning your financial future. One of the possibilities is that you might die sooner than you expect. Should this happen, what challenges will your family face?

Final Expenses

First, there would be certain final expenses: medical and funeral expenses, estate taxes and perhaps probate costs.

Medical expenses vary widely, depending partly on the length of your illness and insurance coverage. The costs can be shockingly high and, unless you die quickly, they also can be overwhelming.

No one knows what the future has in store.

Funeral expenses, which vary from one area of the country to another, can be determined by inquiring at a funeral home. A traditional burial averages $4,000, while a cemetery plot and headstone can boost the cost by thousands more.

The federal government imposes an estate tax on that portion of your estate which exceeds $600,000 after deducting such matters as funeral expenses, debts, a marital deduction and charitable gifts. In addition, most states impose inheritance taxes. The exemptions and rates vary from state to state.

Settling an estate through probate court can be costly, but the impact of estate taxes and probate costs can often be reduced by efficient estate planning and by **having a current will**. Obviously, the services of a competent attorney would be beneficial in this regard.

If you knew you were going to die tomorrow, you would be faced with at least two other related financial challenges **today**: first, to provide enough cash to take care of your survivors, and second, to make provisions for money management.

How Much Money Is Needed to Provide for Your Survivors' Future?

Before you can answer this question, consider:

- **What do you want your family to have?**
- **How much income is needed each month?**
- **Where can this money come from?**
- **How much cash is required today to provide the extra income for the future?**

◆ What do you want your family to have?

Do you want to provide your family with the same standard of living they are accustomed to? Do you want them to be able to remain in the same neighborhood? If you have children, do you want them to attend the same schools? Do you want them to have the college education you had planned? The answers are important, because they will help you determine what you want your family to have if you should die unexpectedly.

◆ How much income is needed each month?

To determine the monthly amount for your survivors, certain assumptions must be made. First, assume living costs will be the same in the future as they are today (these costs can be adjusted later).

Second, assume your family will continue to live in the same home. There are enough variables without changing homes.

How do you estimate the income it will take to provide what you want your family to have? First, determine how much it costs each month for you and your family to live. Of course, if you were to die tomorrow, some of the expenses would be reduced. For example, the food and clothing bills would be less and, most likely, the dental and medical bills would be reduced.

If you have children, money will probably be needed for their college education. The average tuition, room and board for college at a state university in 1991 was nearly $5,000 a year. Over a four-year period, this amounts to approximately $20,000 (in today's dollars) for each child. Private schools are much more expensive, averaging four times as much.

If you have children, money will be needed for their college education.

◆ Where can this money come from?

The income you want your survivors to have can come from several sources, including:

Social Security benefits
Interest on savings
Income from investments
Insurance annuity income
Your spouse's salary
Family aid

If you have dependent children, Social Security benefits will make a good foundation for their support. In most cases, however, this income is not enough to meet all living and educational expenses, so one or more of the above sources must be tapped.

◆ How much CASH is required TODAY to provide the needed income for the future?

The following case study is intended to help you understand the process of determining how much cash it might take. Of course, your personal situation may be different and the amount of cash you might need can vary greatly from the assumptions outlined below.

Fixed Assumptions:

You are age 40 and married.

Your wife is 38.

Your wife will stop working.

You have determined that if you die you want your wife to have $2,000 each month (in today's dollars) for life.

Variable Assumptions:

Changes in the average annual rate of return on investments

Social Security payments

Inflation

Providing for two children and their college education

Four different tables are presented. The first table is fully explained in order to help you understand the other three.

Let's assume first, as illustrated in Table 8-1, that in addition to the fixed assumptions, the variable assumptions are set as follows:

The rate of return can vary from 0% to 16%.

You are **not** covered by Social Security.

There will be **no** inflation.

You have **no** children.

Notice that the amount on the 0% line is not only equal to the amount needed to provide what you want if uninvested – **it is also equal** to the total amount of money that would be paid to your beneficiaries over time.

(8-1)
IF YOU DIE
How Much Cash Does It Take At Age 40 to Provide
$2,000 Monthly in Today's Dollars for Your Wife, Age 38?

NO Social Security / Inflation / Children   **WIFE'S AGE ENDING**

(%)	70	80	90	100
0	$768,000	$1,008,000	$1,248,000	$1,488,000
4	436,823	493,275	531,445	557,232
6	347,219	375,337	391,038	399,805
8	284,363	298,579	305,164	308,214
10	238,932	246,232	249,047	250,134
12	205,164	208,968	210,193	210,587
14	179,425	181,433	181,975	182,124
16	159,313	160,389	160,631	160,685
	32	42	52	62

YEARS COVERED

The table above indicates that it would take $1,488,000 if uninvested to pay your wife, age 38, $2,000 a month until she reaches 100 ($2,000 x 12 months x 62 years = $1,488,000).

If she could receive a 6% rate of return on her money, it would take only $399,805 to pay $2,000 a month to age 100. In other words, it would take only $399,805 invested at the rate of 6% to pay a total of $1,488,000 by age 100. The difference between these two figures is

$1,088,195. This represents the earnings that would be paid on the money invested. It is amazing how the power of compounding multiplies. In this example, your wife would have used up all the money by age 100. Part of the money would come from the principal, but most would come from the earnings.

Suppose your wife could earn 2% more a year?

If your wife were able to earn an 8% average rate of return on the invested money, Table 8-1 indicates it would take only $308,214 today to provide $2,000 a month to her until she is age 100. During those 62 years, she would receive a total of $1,488,000. Of this amount, $1,179,786 would have been from earnings on the money. Note that there is little difference in the amount of money necessary to provide to age 100 than to provide to age 80. It would cost only $9,635 more to provide $2,000 a month for another 20 years ($308,214 - $298,579 = $9,635).

Suppose your wife bought an insurance annuity.

There is another way for your wife to receive $2,000 a month, and that is through an insurance annuity. For a certain premium, an insurance company will guarantee a fixed payment of $2,000 a month to your wife for the rest of her life or to her beneficiary for a minimum guaranteed premium period of 240 months (20 years). The one-time premium required by the insurance company for an annuity to guarantee payment of $2,000 a month to your wife, age 38, for life is $326,018.* It makes no difference how long she might live. If your wife should die one month after receiving the first check, the insurance company would pay her beneficiary 239 more monthly checks of $2,000. This **does not mean** that the insurance company would pay your wife's beneficiary a lump sum payment of $478,000 (239 times $2,000). It would pay only the present value of $2,000 a month for 239 months. That figure, in this case, using 8% for instance, would be $243,726. As you can see, if your wife died during the first month, **the estate would have lost $82,292 for the guarantee of receiving $2,000 a month for her life** ($326,018 - $243,726 = $82,292).

*Source: Immediate Annuity from Manufacturers' Life Insurance Company.

Now let's consider what effect Social Security benefits would have on the amount of cash needed. If Social Security benefits compensate for a portion of the monthly amount needed, how much cash would it take to provide the remaining amount for your wife? The figures are shown in the table below. In our case study using 6%, the cash needed now is $359,079. Social Security benefits have reduced the amount by $40,726 ($399,805 - $359,079 = $40,726).

(8-2)
IF YOU DIE
How Much Cash Does It Take At Age 40 to Provide
$2,000 Monthly in Today's Dollars for Your Wife, Age 38?

Receiving Social Security
NO Inflation
Children

(%)	WIFE'S AGE ENDING 70	80	90	100
0	$702,060	$810,180	$918,300	$1,026,420
4	416,042	441,494	458,687	470,302
6	335,387	348,055	355,128	359,079
8	277,532	283,937	286,904	288,279
10	234,948	238,237	239,506	239,995
12	202,814	204,528	205,077	205,254
14	178,025	178,930	179,174	179,240
16	158,472	158,956	159,067	159,091
	32	42	52	62

YEARS COVERED

The Social Security benefits to your wife without children
amounted to $1,099 a month after age 65.

Besides considering Social Security, consider next what effect 4% inflation would have on the amount of cash needed now. If the cost of living increases an average of 4% each year (this could be higher or lower), the amount of cash needed today (using 6%) is more than double the amount in the first case study. These figures are shown in the following table ($848,817 vs. $399,805 from Table 8-1).

(8-3)   *IF YOU DIE*
How Much Cash Does It Take At Age 40 to Provide
$2,000 Monthly in Today's Dollars for Your Wife, Age 38?

Receiving Social Security
Assuming 4% Inflation Yearly
NO Children

WIFE'S AGE ENDING

(%)	70	80	90	100
0	$1,485,880	$2,427,516	$3,910,860	$6,209,280
4	750,333	968,895	1,201,436	1,444,955
6	563,716	671,592	766,580	848,817
8	437,977	492,137	531,708	560,131
10	350,901	378,515	395,315	405,361
12	288,900	303,190	310,454	314,080
14	243,558	251,058	254,254	255,590
16	209,552	213,545	214,974	215,477
	32	42	52	62

YEARS COVERED

The Social Security benefits to your wife without children
amounted to $1,099 a month after age 65.

Table 8-4 shows the impact of including two children, ages 13 and 11, and providing $4,733 a year for four years (in today's dollars) for each child's college education. Even though two children and college expenses have been included in this table, notice that the figures **are less** than the corresponding figures in Table 8-3, which does **not include** any children. Why is this? Social Security benefits to your wife with children amounted to $1,922 a month initially for the first five years and $824 a month for two additional years until both the 13-year-old and the 11-year-old reach 18. These payments (using 6%) reduce the need for cash ($767,843 vs. $848,817).

These tables give you an idea of **how much cash it would take today** to provide what you want, using various assumptions. Of course, these figures may not apply in your case. You may not be 40. Your wife may

(8-4)   *IF YOU DIE*
How Much Cash Does It Take At Age 40 to Provide
$2,000 Monthly in Today's Dollars for Your Wife, Age 38?

Receiving Social Security Benefits
Assuming 4% Inflation Yearly
$4,733 Yearly for College Education
For Each Child, Ages 11 and 13

WIFE'S AGE ENDING

(%)	70	80	90	100
0	$1,400,208	$2,341,836	$3,825,180	$6,123,600
4	667,804	886,166	1,118,707	1,362,226
6	482,742	590,618	685,606	767,843
8	358,862	413,022	452,593	481,016
10	273,699	301,313	318,113	328,159
12	213,636	227,926	235,190	238,816
14	170,228	177,728	180,924	182,260
16	138,137	142,130	143,559	144,062
	32	42	52	62

YEARS COVERED

The Social Security benefits to your wife with children amounted to $1,922
a month for 5 years until the oldest child reaches 18, and $824 a month
for two more years until the youngest child reaches 18,
and then $1,099 a month after age 65.

not be 38. Your Social Security benefits may be larger or smaller than those shown in this example. The rate of inflation, number and ages of your children and their expected college costs will be different from those used. The most accurate way to determine what it would take to provide all of what you want is to find a reliable computer service that can calculate the numbers based upon the information you supply.

A service, available to you, is discussed later. It provided the calculations for the data in this chapter.

In most cases the best insurance policy
for you is the least profitable for the agent.

Where Can the Money Come From?

The best insurance may well be the least expensive.

In the event of your death, a good source of extra money for your family can come from **Pure Permanent Annual Renewable Term Life Insurance**. Because it costs relatively little today to buy all the protection you want, there is no need to be under-insured. Insurance need not be expensive if you buy the right kind – that is, if you get your money's worth.

Insurance need not be expensive if you buy the right kind – that is, if you get your money's worth.

Life Insurance

In a time when millions of people spend billions on life insurance, it is startling how few have any real understanding of what they are buying and what they should expect from their insurance.

This lack of knowledge can be explained partially by the reliance on a life insurance agent for facts. In addition to performing a service for you, the agent has an interest in selling a policy and earning a commission. The higher the cost of a policy, the greater the company's profit and the higher the commission paid to the agent. In most cases, the best insurance policy for you is the least profitable for the agent.

Insurance companies are under no legal requirement to disclose all the facts. Policies are almost always sold as a package – a certain face dollar amount for a certain premium. You are seldom informed about how much of your premium payment goes to the agent as commission, how much is going to the company and how much is being spent for actual insurance protection. This is unlike the securities industry which is required by the government to provide full disclosure of important facts, including all costs and commissions.

Insurance policies
are almost always
sold as a package.

If you clearly understand the concept of when you need life insurance, how much and what kind gives you the most protection for your
money, and how long you need to keep it, you do not have to be told by
anyone what you should or should not do. But what if you don't fully
understand the concept?

When should you buy life insurance?

If you are not worried about the consequences of dying prematurely,
why waste **any** of your money on life insurance?

The odds are good that you **will live** beyond 65. If you are confident
that you will exceed that age, why carry any insurance? Why not cancel
all of your life insurance policies? If you are not worried about dying,
why waste your money on life insurance? Why pay any premiums at all?
Why not use the money to "live a little" today and enjoy life more?

You would probably say, "I can't do that – I might die before then."
So ask yourself – "**when** might I die?" This is one of the most important
questions that you must ask yourself. Be fair, and answer it rationally.

Look at **your life line** in the chart below, and check off the time you believe that you might die. Take time now to determine your **end of the line**.

(9-1)   *Your Life Line*

Again, if you are not worried about dying until 10 years from today, why carry any life insurance now? Why not drop all of your policies, save money, and stack those dollars on top of one another for your future? Aren't there more enjoyable ways of spending your money? Just before your **end of the line**, why not buy a huge policy and leave your family well off?

When should you buy life insurance?

Again, you will no doubt say, "I can't do that...I might die before then." But when? Aren't you carrying life insurance **now** because you are worried that you might die **tonight** – not 10 years in the future or at age 65 – but **tonight**? If you understand this concept, you will never have any difficulty deciding **when** you should have insurance on your life.

Let's illustrate this point in another, less emotional way – using **fire insurance**, something most of us buy wisely.

You have the fire insurance because you are worried that you might have a fire tonight, not five or 10 years in the future, but tonight.

If you own a home you carry fire insurance, don't you? You don't believe your house will burn to the ground – but it **could** happen. You have the fire insurance because you are worried that you might have a fire **tonight**, not five or 10 years in the future, but tonight. **Why not carry the same reasoning over to your consideration of life insurance**?

The First Year of Our Marriage

During the first few months of our marriage, my wife and I wondered if I should have life insurance to protect her if I died and, if so, how much. At the time, I was 30 years old and had one $10,000 policy on my life which my mother had purchased several years earlier. We determined life insurance was not needed, because of the money we had saved and invested. We were both unwilling to pay the $210 premium due on the existing policy. It was better to invest the $210 each year than spend it on life insurance. We terminated the policy and gave the cash value of $900 back to my mother.

We decided it was wiser to buy a large amount of life insurance when we had children. Therefore, when we were expecting

*our first child in 1956, we bought $200,000 worth of life insurance
on my life. Ordinary life insurance for $200,000 would have cost us
$3,200 in annual premiums. Instead we bought annual renewable
term insurance with a premium cost of only $926 each year. The
term policy provided the most protection for the least amount of
money and saved us $2,274 that year alone ($3,200 - $926 =
$2,274). (More about annual renewable term insurance later.)*

Assets Needed for Survivors' Security

The bottom line in the following chart is drawn to represent your
LIFE LINE. It begins with NOW at the left and extends into your future
toward the right. Above this line is drawn your Survivors' Security Line.
This represents the assets needed, in the event of your death, to provide
your family with the necessary income. It is highest NOW and decreases
as time passes. For example, 10 years from today, your children will be 10
years older, 10 years further through school, 10 years closer (you hope) to
being self-supporting. Your spouse will be 10 years older and will have 10
years' worth of living expenses already paid. For these reasons, the need
for Survivors' Security decreases with each passing year.

(9-2)   *Assets Needed for Survivors' Security*

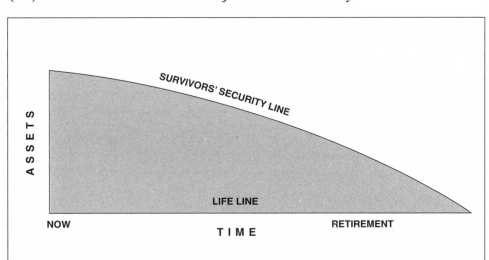

On the other hand, your goal of being financially independent is separate and distinct from your Survivors' Security. In the next chart, your LIFE LINE is again drawn from NOW into your future. Above your LIFE LINE is your Financial Independence Line. This represents the total assets you plan to accumulate in the future for yourself and your family. You want the amount to increase from NOW, so that you will achieve your goal of being financially independent at retirement. This is your own goal…**to be financially independent**.

(9-3)   *Assets You Accumulate…Toward Financial Independence*

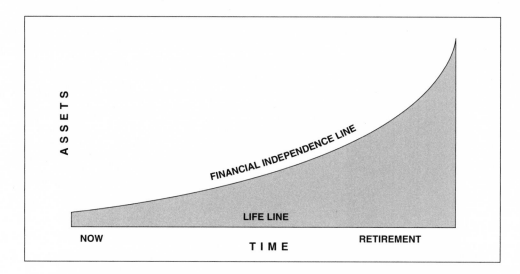

If you superimpose your Survivors' Security Line over your Financial Independence line, you can clearly visualize how much extra money is needed to provide for your family in the event of your death today.

As Chart 9-4 indicates, in the event of your premature death, a portion of the money your family will need can come from the assets you already have accumulated. Initially, though, most of it will probably have to come from life insurance or from some other outside source.

As time passes, your Survivors' Security Line decreases, while your Financial Independence Line (your accumulated assets) increases. The darker shaded area indicates the total amount of extra money you need for your survivors' security beyond the amount you have already accumulated. That extra amount indicates the amount of insurance you should probably have. As you can see, the amount of insurance necessary to provide for your Survivors' Security decreases with the passage of time.

(9-4)   *The Extra Assets Needed*

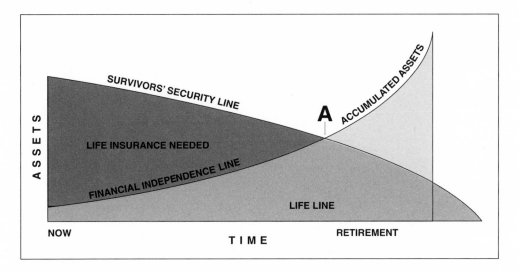

When point A in the chart above is reached, the assets you have accumulated are exactly equal to the amount of money you want for your survivors' security. At this point, you are fully **self-insured** through **your own** investments. Accordingly, there is no need for any outside insurance money from that point on. Instead of wasting money on life insurance premiums from Point A until your retirement, why not invest all of the premiums in order to reach your financial goal earlier? This could mean an earlier retirement or more luxurious lifestyle for your family. But until you reach Point A, you will probably need some insurance to protect your family.

If you knew you were going to die tonight…

If you knew you were going to die tonight:

	ANSWER
When would you buy life insurance?	Now
How much life insurance would you buy?	As much as I could
How much would you be willing to pay?	Least amount possible

According to some insurance agents, you have one reason for buying insurance, while your neighbor, who is the same age, has quite a different reason. For $1,000 worth of protection you are convinced to pay one price, your neighbor another. For the same amount of insurance at age 35, one of you pays an annual premium of $2.43, the other, an annual premium of $60. If both of you die, your survivors will receive a check for the same amount of money, $1,000. The higher the premium, the more the protection costs. The only difference in the amount you pay depends upon how informed you are and what **you are willing to pay** for the same life insurance benefit.

The notion that the higher the premium, the greater the protection, is not necessarily true. Assuming all insurance companies have the same financial stability, **the best insurance may well be the least expensive**.

There is one type of policy that gives you the most protection for the least amount of money. It offers protection only – no savings or cash value – only pure insurance. This is one of the policies used by life insurance companies when they buy and sell insurance among themselves. This is the **Pure Permanent Annual Renewable Term** life insurance policy. It is **pure** because it provides only insurance protection; it is not an investment since it has no cash value. It is **permanent** because the insurance is guaranteed renewable for life. Your actual cost for this insurance rises along with the expected mortality cost to the life insurance company. Most other life insurance policies have much higher costs each year **for life**. The premium rate of the policy is determined by adding an expense and profit factor to the cost derived from the life insurance mortality table. **As the mortality cost increases, so does the premium rate necessary for that age** (i.e., the older you get, the greater probability that you are going to die).

(9-5)   *Premium Rates for each $1,000 of Insurance*

Pure Permanent Annual Renewable Term

Attained Age	Premium per $1,000	Attained Age	Premium per $1,000	Attained Age	Premium per $1,000	Attained Age	Premium per $1,000
20	$1.73	40	$ 3.42	60	$19.66	80	$106.27
21	1.77	41	3.72	61	21.49	81	115.32
22	1.80	42	4.03	62	23.49	82	124.81
23	1.83	43	4.38	63	25.68	83	134.67
24	1.85	44	4.76	64	28.06	84	144.94
25	1.87	45	5.17	65	30.68	85	155.70
26	1.90	46	5.64	66	33.57	86	166.98
27	1.93	47	6.15	67	36.76	87	178.87
28	1.97	48	6.72	68	40.28	88	191.55
29	2.01	49	7.35	69	44.07	89	205.28
30	2.06	50	8.04	70	48.11	90	220.43
31	2.12	51	8.81	71	52.32	91	237.46
32	2.18	52	9.63	72	56.67	92	256.94
33	2.25	53	10.53	73	61.13	93	279.52
34	2.32	54	11.50	74	65.82	94	305.95
35	2.43	55	.12.57	75	70.89	95	339.36
36	2.56	56	13.73	76	76.51	96	387.02
37	2.71	57	15.02	77	82.87	97	471.90
38	2.91	58	16.43	78	89.92	98	645.56
39	3.15	59	17.97	79	97.77		

The premium rates in the chart above are from a policy issued by our Survivors' Benefit Insurance Company which we sold in 1980. These rates are comparable to rates that can be found with other life insurance companies today. Notice how slowly the premiums rise from year to year.

The premium rates for $1,000 worth of insurance are graphed to scale in the chart below. Superimposed upon this graph is an appropriate **Need for Protection** line.

(9-6)   *Annual Renewable Term Life Insurance*

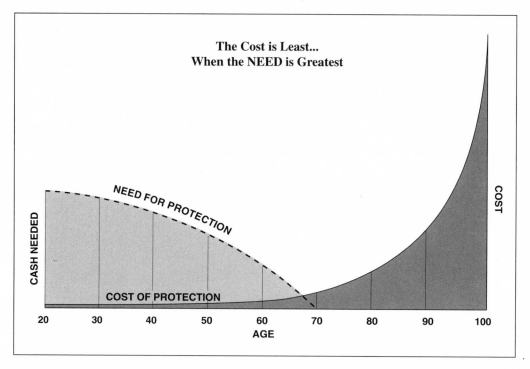

The cost goes up each year **along with** the mortality cost on a very gradual basis. **The cost of protection is least when the need for it is greatest**.

Annual renewable term life insurance can be described as a **"pay-as-you-go, get-what-you-pay-for"** policy. If you are 35 years old, you are not required to pay today the higher cost required at age 60 or even age 36. You can pay that higher rate **if and when** you arrive at that age.

Who buys annual renewable term life insurance? Usually there are only three groups of people who do:

Those who completely understand insurance.

Those who have limited funds and cannot afford expensive insurance.

Those who are getting their money's worth without knowing it.

Money Management

Money Management

*The biggest challenge of money management
is how to make money with money.*

Even if you are able to provide your survivors with the cash they will need, is this all you need to do?

For example, if you die unexpectedly, in addition to experiencing the shock of your death, your widow, who does not have much experience in managing money, will be faced with many decisions. Besides taking care of the funeral arrangements, taxes, doctor bills, calming herself and reassuring the family, your widow will be contacted by a representative of one of your insurance companies. Actually, she doesn't want to talk to anyone, but the financial situation demands it.

Even if you are able to provide your survivors with the cash they will need, is this all you need to do?

The agent tells your widow how much insurance you provided for her. He asks her what she wants to do with the money. Not being sure what to do, she asks the agent for advice. The agent suggests an insurance annuity that would pay her a definite sum each month for the rest of her life. "The money will never run out," the agent says, and encourages her to do this. Because she is upset and does not want to make any major financial decisions quickly, she tells the agent she wants to think about it. At this point, she is not certain what she should do. She is anxious and confused.

Next, she might seek advice from close friends. They might explain that an insurance annuity is not the answer because it does not protect her against future inflation. They tell her there will be no way to obtain additional cash in case of an emergency. Instead of an insurance annuity, they recommend that she take all the money from the insurance company and deposit it in several different savings and loan associations. They feel she will earn more money from her investment that way. She listens to what they say, but is still undecided.

Your widow tells your
doctor about her
financial problems
and asks advice.

Perhaps your family doctor calls on your widow. During the conversation, she tells your doctor about her financial problems and asks advice. The doctor advises her to invest in mutual funds and let professionals manage the money.

This sounds logical but she is not ready to make financial decisions, and she continues to seek advice.

An enterprising broker reads of your death and contacts your widow. Again, she solicits advice. The broker suggests she take the money in cash and permit him to invest it, indicating that her problems will then be solved. She will have no more decisions to make; they will be made for her. But she still has questions.

While discussing the settlement of your estate with her attorney, your widow reveals her problem. The attorney suggests that she create a trust and allow a bank trust department to administer it for her.

No wonder your widow is confused. Everyone she has talked with has given her different advice. She feels that some of her advisers are looking out for their own best interests. She realizes that this might be the largest lump sum of money she will ever receive, and she is afraid of making the wrong decision and losing money. Because she remains confused, she does nothing. She tells the insurance company to pay the money to her in cash. She deposits the money in her checking account and then waits, hoping that somehow a decision will be made for her.

Several years later, your widow confides in a close friend: "I am worried about my money. I am not sure what to do. **I wish my husband and I had discussed this while he was still alive**."

Is providing enough money for your survivors all you should do? Of course not. Why not discuss your opinions with your wife and make a plan together while you both still are alive?

Before you agree on a plan, why not first consider the challenges of money management? There are two fundamental issues:

- **Spending Money Wisely**
- **Making Money with Money**

◆ Spending Money Wisely

Most people spend money wisely, trying to get their money's worth. If you and your wife fall into this category, you do not have a problem. If you believe there may be a problem, perhaps you can both agree to control the amount of money that will be available to spend by using a trust instrument or an insurance annuity.

Trust Instrument

If you are worried about your wife's ability to manage the spending of money, or if you want to limit the amount of money your wife can spend, you can have your attorney establish a trust instrument now. In this legal document, you can give a trustee the power to control the

If you are worried about your wife's ability to manage the spending of money...

spending of the assets. The trustee can be an individual or the trust department of a bank. If a trust is used, your wife will usually be given a fixed amount of money to spend. If your wife runs low on money or has a financial crisis, she can ask for more. The trustee will charge a fee for this non-investment management service. It should be pointed out that it is unlikely that a trustee will be willing to perform this service only. The trustee will most likely ask to be given the right to make investment decisions as well and charge an additional fee.

Advantage of having a trustee:

Impartial control of spending

Disadvantages of using a trustee:

Your wife may be at the mercy of the trustee even if she is a co-trustee in the document. If additional money is needed your wife must try to convince the trustee. If she wants additional funds for anything, she must, in a sense, "beg" for the money. (This could be avoided if the trust allowed discretionary withdrawals.)

You may think that the fee required by the trustee for this service is not reasonable. You're probably right.

Insurance Annuity

Another way to control the spending of money would be to have your wife buy an insurance annuity. As discussed above, the annuity is a contract issued by a life insurance company that guarantees a specific monthly payment for life.

Advantages of an insurance annuity:

Your wife will receive a fixed income each month for life.

Your wife will not need to be worried about money management.

Disadvantages of an insurance annuity:

The annuity does not provide for protection against any loss in the value of a dollar.

No extra cash is available. If there were an emergency requiring extra cash, the money could not be obtained from the insurance company.

An insurance annuity is expensive. It takes a great deal of cash to provide a guaranteed monthly payment for life.

If your wife dies early, the value of her estate will be reduced.

◆ Making Money with Money

The biggest challenge of money management is how to make money with money. To make money with money, many decisions must be made. Someone must decide **where** to put the money to work, **how much** should be put in any one place, and **when** the money should be taken out and placed somewhere else. And those decisions must be made continually.

The biggest challenge of money management is how to make money with money.

Let's examine just three choices concerning who can make these money management decisions:

> **Your Wife**
> **A Trust Department**
> **A Fully-Managed Mutual Fund**

Your Wife Can Make Decisions

Your wife can listen to the suggestions of others, read financial periodicals, then take chances with individual security investments. As with anyone making financial decisions, investment success will be a function of her education, her experience in money matters, and her ability to make the correct decisions. You need to consider the potential anxiety level associated with this choice.

A Trust Department

If your wife is not confident about making investment decisions, she can go to a bank trust department for money management. For a fee, the trustee will perform this service. For additional fees, a trust department will perform other services.

Advantages of having a trust department make investment decisions:

Offers professional experience in money management

Removes the responsibility of money management from your wife's shoulders

Makes investment decisions according to your instructions

One advantage of having a trust department manage your money is that… investment decisions are made according to your instructions.

Disadvantages of using a trust department to manage money:

Generally, a trust department can offer only part-time investment management. For example, let's assume a trust department has 500 individual trust accounts. Let's also assume that there are 10 trust officers to manage these accounts. If the accounts were divided equally, each of the officers would have 50 accounts. If a trust officer spends equal time on each of his 50 accounts during a year, each account will receive the equivalent of only five working days of personal investment management a year. Actually, the time may not be divided this way. The larger accounts will undoubtedly command more time and the smaller accounts will receive less time.

The quality of a trust department's work depends on several factors: first, upon the **ability** of the particular investment adviser, and second, upon how much **time** the trust officer spends with your wife's trust account. No matter how intelligent the trust officer, the quality of work cannot be good unless adequate time is spent on the account.

The investment management given by a trust department is generally overly conservative. With the continued erosion in the value of a dollar, this conservative stance could adversely affect long-term investment results.

The past investment record of individual trusts of a trust department is not generally available to the public.

A Fully-Managed Mutual Fund

If your wife does not want to make the individual investment decisions, the money can be managed by a **fully-managed mutual fund**. This type of fund is one in which the investment manager is given the broadest authority possible at all times to use his best judgment in managing the fund's assets as to:

The past investment record of individual trusts of a trust department is generally not available to the public.

What to invest in.

How much to invest in a particular security.

How long to remain invested.

How much cash should be held if more attractive investments cannot be found.

Advantages of having a fully-managed mutual fund:

A fund provides full-time rather than part-time management.

An established mutual fund has the means and is willing to hire excellent management personnel.

More investment management is received for each dollar paid.

No matter if your account is big or small, all investors get the same attention from the fund's management.

All the manager's time is spent taking care of one portfolio of securities. More time is spent making investment decisions, so there is greater opportunity for better results.

Detailed record keeping is provided.

The performance record is public and the results are audited.

Disadvantages of a fully-managed mutual fund:

Most of these funds invest only in marketable securities. Because of this, closely held companies and personal real estate investments cannot be used since they are not marketable.

No individual investment advice is given since the mutual fund is managed for all fund investors.

Test drive your financial plan.

"Test Drive" Your Financial Plan

If you believe that the trust department of a bank is the best place for your wife's money to be managed after you are gone, tell her **now**. If the trust department is good enough for your wife, why isn't it also good enough for you? Why not give the bank's trust department a chance to manage your money today? See what the bank can do with it and at what cost. If you are not satisfied now, why should your wife be satisfied later?

If you decide mutual funds can best serve your family's financial needs, discuss it with your wife **now**. Tomorrow may be too late.

Try investing some of your money in selected mutual funds. See what the results are. Find out what other services are offered. See if you are satisfied with what mutual funds **can do for you now**. Your family will benefit in the future from the experiences you gain today.

PART

4

Planning for Financial Independence

Introduction to Investing

Introduction to Investing

There is no such thing as a perfectly safe investment,
free from all risk.

If you want the financial freedom in the future to do what you want to do when you want to do it, you must begin to trade your money for something that can grow in value over time and/or will generate income. **This is investing**.

When considering investing, most people think primarily of putting their money to work productively. They look to their assets to provide a source of independent income – a second income – separate from work income.

No person is free, in an economic sense, who does not have adequate investment income entirely unrelated to work. A person earning $100,000 a year, without a nickel in investments to show for it, has less freedom than a person who earns a moderate wage but who owns income-producing assets paying $10,000 annually.

No person is free, in an economic sense, who does not have adequate investment income entirely unrelated to work.

One of the prime objectives of a sound investment program is to place the responsibility for protecting your investment on someone else's shoulders – someone experienced in managing money.

Perhaps no one appreciates the need for having investment income without the responsibility of management more than the owner of a small business. The more successful the business, the more dependent it is on every ounce of the owner's energy. It is as though the owner has the proverbial tiger by the tail and dares not let go. Sooner or later, every small business owner comes to realize that the degree of genuine financial success that the owner can enjoy is best measured by the amount of assets that are invested in someone else's business, often through the medium of common stocks.

There is another significant reason why you should be interested in delegating the investment management function: you accumulate investments not only for your own benefit, but also for your survivors. To the extent that your investments require your personal supervision – your ideas, planning, and judgment – it may not be desirable to have them taken over by your survivors who are much less familiar than you are with managing them.

It may not be desirable to have your investments taken over by your survivors who are much less familiar than you are with managing them.

How Investments Can Earn Money:

Appreciation – The increase in value of assets such as stocks, bonds, commodities or real estate

Dividends – Income received as an owner of a business

Interest – Income received from lending your money

Capital Gains – Profits received from the sale of assets

Basic Attributes of Attractive Investments

Some of the basic attributes investors look for in an attractive investment include:

- ◆ **Professional Management**
- ◆ **Income Production**
- ◆ **Capital Growth Opportunity**
- ◆ **Availability in Convenient Amounts**
- ◆ **Ease of Transfer of Ownership**
- ◆ **Liquidity (ease of sale)**
- ◆ **Acceptability as Collateral for a Loan**
- ◆ **Limited Liability**
- ◆ **Inflation Hedge**

◆ Professional Management

Professional management means transferring the responsibility to someone who is qualified to free you of day-to-day, time-consuming research and decisions relating to investments so that you can continue to devote your efforts to succeed in your chosen work.

◆ Income Production

The investment provides the possibility of ongoing income payments without the sale of capital assets. For example, investing in diamonds is not a good choice because they would not produce income. Only by selling them could you receive cash.

◆ Capital Growth Opportunity

You may seek an investment vehicle that offers the opportunity for your investment to grow in value.

◆ Availability in Convenient Amounts

Can the investment be purchased in comparatively small amounts at different times, such as shares of common stocks, or does it require a substantial immediate investment, such as a home?

◆ Ease of Transfer of Ownership

It is desirable to be able to easily transfer your interest in your investment to someone else, whether by sale or gift. Your options are extremely limited if you do not have this privilege.

◆ Liquidity

You want an active public market for your investments so that, should you decide to sell, you do not have to seek out an individual buyer. The importance of liquidity cannot be overemphasized. One of the advantages of being a stockholder in a publicly owned corporation is marketability – the ability to readily sell your stock.

◆ Acceptability as Collateral

You may have a temporary need for funds to meet an emergency or to take advantage of an opportunity. You do not want to sell your investment but simply borrow against it. Naturally, the ease with which it may be used as collateral for a loan contributes to the attractiveness of your investment. If a ready market exists for it, the lender will probably act much more favorably.

◆ Limited Liability

Most people are reluctant to own an investment in which their liability extends beyond the amount of money they have invested.

◆ Inflation Hedge

Your investment should have a good likelihood of appreciating in value to an amount equal to or greater than the loss in value of a dollar, so that it will keep up with the ongoing increases in costs of goods and services.

The Risks of Investing

Nothing is safe in an absolute sense. To think otherwise is to fool oneself. For example, each of us can and should drive our car carefully, but this in itself does not rule out the possibility of an accident, because we cannot control the actions of other drivers on the road.

Likewise, **there is no such thing as a perfectly safe investment**. It is not possible to insulate your financial plan from the effects of national and world economic events. We are living in a dynamic, fast-moving age, and every economic change that occurs can affect us in our pocketbooks.

Smart people do not seek to avoid risks, but simply try to hold them within reasonable limits. **Progress is not possible without risk**. No one can expect success to be guaranteed fully and completely in advance. In fact, experience indicates that those who painstakingly attempt to avoid all financial risks, seeking only "sure" things, face the greatest risk of all – the shrinking value of a dollar.

The two major investment risks involved in the accumulation or conservation of capital are:

- **Loss of principal**
- **Loss in the value of your dollars**

There is no savings or investment plan that is not subject to loss on one or both of these possibilities.

- **Loss of principal** requires little amplification. Any form of savings that does not guarantee to return to you at least the same number of dollars initially saved, anytime you want it, involves the possibility of losing principal. Guarantees are only as good as the financial strength of the organization standing behind them.

- **Loss in the value of your dollars** occurs when a dollar buys fewer goods and services than it did at a previous time.

In summary... **A loss in dollar value is just as real as a loss of principal. In fact, over time, the shrinking value of your dollars can be your greater loss.**

Guarantees are only as good as the financial strength of the organization standing behind them.

No one knowingly makes an investment
with the objective of losing money.

Types of Investments

*No one knowingly makes an investment
with the objective of losing money.*

If you want to put your money to work, you can either lend it to others or you can trade your dollars to own something. If you put your money to work, how much should you expect to make on your investment? If you are not sure how much your money can earn, it is easy to find out. **Just try to borrow money.** See how much you will have to pay to borrow it. This is a good indication of how much you should receive for your money.

...put your money
to work...

There is a marked difference between being a **lender** and an **owner**. Both lenders and owners invest dollars for the same basic purpose: to earn more dollars. Only the approach to the objective is different.

"Lender" Investments

Your primary concern when you lend money is the safety of the loan. Will the borrower be able to pay you the interest on time and repay the obligation in full when it matures?

A secondary consideration is the amount of interest a borrower agrees to pay you for the use of your money.

Here are some examples of loan-type investments:

- **Savings accounts** – When you establish a savings account, you actually lend money. The institution agrees to pay you a stipulated rate of interest on the funds and generally makes them available to you when you want them.

- **Bonds** – A bond is merely the evidence of a loan – an interest-bearing certificate issued by a government or business. When you buy a bond, you are in effect lending your money to an organization or a government which promises to pay you a specified sum (interest) on specific dates and pay back your loan at maturity.

Consider some of the things that are NOT ordinarily a concern to you as a lender:

- You are not concerned about **how** the funds will be used. It is true that you want the borrower's business to prosper so that he will be able to make the interest payments to you as they fall due and, ultimately, to repay the entire loan. But, beyond that, your concern as a lender ceases. Likewise, when receiving 5% on your money from a bank, you are not really concerned about whether the bank earns 2%, 4%, or 8% on the funds you have advanced.

- As a lender, you play the role of a spectator. As long as the borrower continues to honor the terms of the contract, you have no voice in the borrower's operation.

- Only when a borrower fails to fulfill the terms of a contract, for example, by not paying the interest or principal when due, are you given the right to take an active part in the borrower's affairs.

- In theory, you as a lender do not share in the success or the failure, profits or losses of the borrower. In actual practice, of course, the losses (if they are sufficiently severe) can adversely affect your financial position. The savings and loan disaster of recent years is an excellent example of such an event.

Again remember: **There is no such thing as a completely risk-free investment!**

"Owner" Investments

An owner is one who has acquired the title to real or personal property. Generally, as an owner, you are interested in the safety of your principal and the production of investment income. As an owner, you willingly assume a greater degree of risk than a lender does in return for certain advantages of ownership.

◆ Risks of Ownership

As an owner, you absorb any losses sustained by your investment. In the event of a business failure, for example, you stand last in line to recover any part of your investment. **All lenders must be paid first**.

As an owner, no one promises to pay you a return on your investment. There are no guarantees or assurances. When making an investment, you may calculate that it will pay a given income. This is purely a matter of personal judgment and is not supported by any contractual understanding. Whether or not the investment will return income to you depends entirely on the profits of the investment.

Profits are generally unpredictable. This is particularly true over extended periods of time. If you were to purchase an apartment building, it would be reasonable to assume that you could determine with some degree of accuracy your beginning gross income from rent after the expenses of servicing and maintaining the property. To make a projection of earnings five or 10 years into the future becomes increasingly more difficult. What can you expect the rents to be at that time? The rate of occupancy? The labor and maintenance costs? Real estate taxes? The variables that affect the level of profits are almost without end, and the attractiveness of your investment hinges on all these variables.

There is no guarantee of the value you will receive for the property if you choose to sell. If you invested $10,000 in U.S. government savings bonds or in a single-premium life insurance policy, you know precisely what the value of your investment is at any given time. If, however, you invested $10,000 in a retail business, you could not accurately predict what you would realize from the sale of the business.

The selling price you will receive for property at any given time depends not only on the worth of the investment itself, but also the uncertainties of the marketplace and on the value of a dollar at that time. For example, the structural integrity of a home clearly affects its value.

...other factors beyond the home itself contribute to its selling price.

But other factors beyond the home itself contribute to its selling price. For instance, what demand will exist for homes at the time you decide to sell? How popular will the neighborhood be? If you are required to sell at a time when market conditions are generally unfavorable, you may receive considerably less for the property than if the sale were held under more ideal conditions.

Direct ownership of real estate for investment purposes fails to satisfy many of the basic attributes of attractive investments:

◆ **As a real estate owner, you cannot completely free yourself from management responsibilities. Although you may delegate certain responsibilities to an agent, you will always be expected to make the important decisions.**

◆ **Direct ownership of real estate is not available in small denominations. While it is true that you can arrange for a small down payment, financing the balance with a mortgage, you are usually required to make a substantial initial investment.**

◆ **Real estate suffers from a lack of guaranteed marketability.**

◆ **Advantages of ownership**

The factors that are responsible for putting you as an owner at a disadvantage under adverse conditions also give you a powerful advantage when conditions are favorable.

An owner receives **all** the profits. There is **no ceiling** imposed on the financial gains you may enjoy, compared with a lender situation where the interest or return is usually fixed.

Your rights as an owner extend to the full worth of the property, less any loan, including any growth in value of the property that increases your assets. As an owner, if you bought a $100,000 property which subsequently became worth $150,000, the value of your ownership would increase 50%. On the other hand, if you are a lender and lend $25,000 on property valued at $100,000 that subsequently increases in value to $150,000, the value of your loan would remain unchanged.

Property owners usually fare better during inflationary periods than lenders do. Property usually maintains its worth while a dollar loses value, because when the value of your dollars shrinks, it takes more of them to trade for the property.

Other examples of ownership include **part ownership, oil and gas interests, art collectibles and common stock**.

Part-Owner Interest

You may own a part of a business without contributing your services or having a voice in the management, with your risk limited to the amount of your investment. Your ownership interest is not generally transferable; there is no public market for it and it is generally not acceptable as collateral for a loan.

Oil and Gas Interests

You may invest your capital in ventures such as oil and gas drilling interests. If a well produces oil, you receive a proportionate share of the income earned. These are highly speculative undertakings that are typically unsuitable for the average investor.

…oil and gas interests…
are highly speculative
and are typically unsuitable
for the average investor.

Art and Collectibles

Earlier, I mentioned the attributes of attractive investments. In the traditional view of investing, art and collectibles are different from other ownership type investments.

You "manage" your collection and hope to realize profits over time. Originally, the reason for trading your dollars for the collection was in part to enjoy possessing something to wear, such as jewelry, or to decorate your home or office. It takes knowledge and personal involvement to invest intelligently in paintings, sculptures, prints, stamps, coins, photographs and other collectibles. Collecting also requires time – time to be informed, time to enjoy the objects and time for them to appreciate in value. There is, of course, a cost beyond the original investment, since you must pay for insurance against fire and theft and for adequate space to display or store your collection.

Collecting can be a lifetime hobby, but the appreciation in value is best understood by collectors and dealers who are aware of the history and keep up with the collectible market. In trading your dollars for a collectible, consider if you will enjoy possessing the object. Whether it appreciates in value or not will depend on your knowledge of the market and perhaps the artist and on the conditions of the economy at the time of some future trade.

Common Stocks

Common stocks of publicly-owned corporations are an investment that has, to a large degree, the best combination of basic investment attributes. You will find a comparison of these attributes of common stocks with other investment opportunities in Table 14-1.

The ownership of a corporation is indicated by "shares" of what is called common stock. Each share represents a fraction of the total ownership. The term **common** is by no means negative; all owners of a corporation are "common" stockholders.

When you trade dollars for common stocks, you have the most to gain from a successful operation and the most to lose from an unsatisfactory one. Common stocks may come closer to offering all the advantages of an ideal investment than any other medium.

One of the best advantages of "owner" investments is that they are free from the shrinking value of a dollar.

You can blindly accept
what others tell you ...

An Unmanaged Investment –
The Dow Jones Industrial Average

*TIME erodes the value of a dollar but
enhances the value of common stocks.*

If you don't want your money tied to the shrinking value of a dollar, you must develop confidence in the wisdom of investing in common stocks. There are two options available if you want to achieve this. You can either blindly accept what others tell you, or you can take time to study and understand the essential facts that can affect you. Only when you understand the facts can you develop confidence in what you believe and why you believe it.

It is unlikely that you would be reading this book if you intended to rely only on other people for advice. My objective is to try to present, in a simple and straightforward way, the essential facts regarding the characteristics, the short-term risks and the long-term opportunities of owning common stocks.

The history of a long investment record in a group of common stocks was needed to uncover these facts. Probably the best example can be taken from the long-term results of the Dow Jones Industrial Average because it includes a 95-year history of an unmanaged investment in a group of common stocks. The Dow is the oldest and most widely quoted stock market indicator which experts believe represents the overall market at any moment in time. It is made up of a selected group of securities used as an indicator of the performance of all common stocks. Accurate data is available as far back as 1897 and is shown in Chart 13-1.

Occasionally, companies are dropped from the Dow when they are no longer considered representative and others are added. Even with that adjustment, the Dow still represents the value of a group of securities that is "unmanaged." There are no investment management service or brokerage costs included in the investment results of the Dow.

Initially, the Dow consisted of 12 securities. In 1916 the number was increased to 20. Then in 1928 it was raised to 30, the number still in use.

(13-1)   ***The Value of the Dow Jones Industrial Average***
on the First Day of Each Quarter From 1897 Through 1991
*(Dividends **Not** Reinvested)*

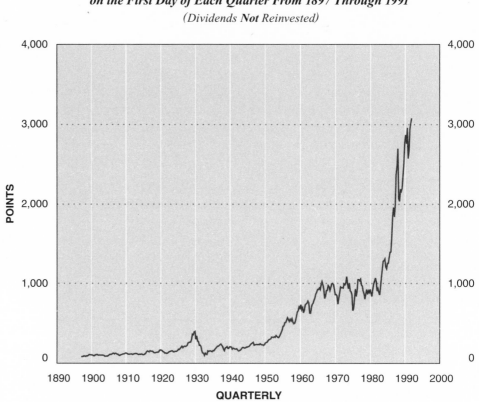

♦ **The Dow's Behavior Over Time**

What should you observe while studying the chart above?

♦ Fluctuations

The value of the Dow fluctuates. Most of the changes are minimal, but occasionally they are dramatic. These major changes, both up and down, are caused mainly by **greed and fear** – emotional reactions to corporate, economic and world news. In good times, people tend to be too optimistic and take the Dow to highs that cannot be supported by reality. In bad times, the tendency is to be too pessimistic (occasionally to the point of panic), which forces the Dow below where it rationally should be.

The value of the Dow fluctuates... occasionally the changes are dramatic.

The Dow moves in cycles, which vary in two ways:
+ Height and depth: Some cycles are much steeper than others.
+ Breadth: Some cycles take much longer to complete than others.

♦ Long-Term Upward Trend

As shown in the chart, the long-term trend of the Dow has been up since 1897. The Dow started at an adjusted value of **29.87** on January 1, 1897. On December 31, 1991, it was **3,168.83**.

♦ Spurts (uneven trends)

The upward trends are uneven. Many of the major moves are in spurts, few of which were predicted.

♦ Always Rising to New Highs

No matter where you point on the chart, since 1897 the Dow has always risen to new highs over time.

The Opportunity of a Lifetime

Where on the chart of the Dow would you have wanted to make an investment if you could have? Most likely at one of the major lows! However, it would be entirely by luck and accident if you were able to determine the exact lows.

If you can't pick the exact lows, would you rather buy when the Dow is going up or going down? Most people buy when the market is going up, but if you buy when it's going down, you just might earn more money over time. There are two reasons for making more money over time. First, each time you buy when the Dow is falling, you receive more shares for each of your dollars. Second, the value of the Dow has always gone to new highs in time. **Your risk comes only if you are forced to sell your shares at a time when the share price is below your cost.** It takes time for the Dow to go to new highs. Thus, the true risk is not enough TIME. Whenever the price of the Dow is at or near a major low, it probably presents you with a great opportunity.

Most people buy when the market is going up, but if you buy when it's going down, you just might earn more money over time.

◆ Value of the Dow Versus a Dollar Over Time

Although one cannot invest directly in the Dow, the following study relates to a hypothetical investment in the Dow. The next chart shows the value of $1 invested in the Dow with all dividends reinvested from 1897 through 1991. This illustrates the total return of the Dow Jones Industrial Average. Superimposed on this chart is the value of a 1900 dollar over time.

This chart indicates that one 1900 dollar ($1.00) kept in a **safe** place could be traded for approximately six cents' ($0.06) worth of goods or services at the end of 1991. On the other hand, if the same dollar had been invested in the unmanaged Dow, it could have been exchanged in 1991 for 8,934 dollars.

The line representing the value of $1 invested in the Dow on January 1, 1897, appears to be close to zero until a little after 1940. This is not as it appears. The actual values at the end of various periods of time are shown in Chart 13-3.

(13-2)   ***The Value of $1 Invested in the Dow From 1897 Through 1991,***
              Compared to the Diminishing Value of a 1900 Dollar
              *(With **All** Dividends Reinvested and Compounded)*

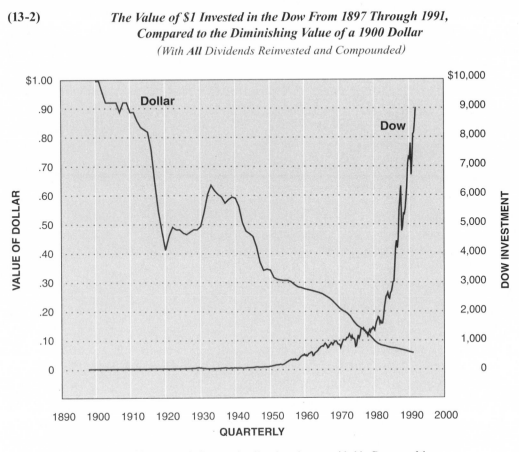

Source: Investors Research Corporation based on data provided by Bureau of the Census and Bureau of Labor Statistics.

Chart 13-3, on the next page, shows that if you multiply the last figure by 10,000, you will determine that $10,000 invested in the Dow on January 1, 1897, with all dividends reinvested and no consideration given for taxes, would have been worth $89,338,300 at the end of December 1991, a 95-year period. The annual average percent return over that period was 10.04%.

(13-3)   *Actual Value of $1 Invested in the Dow on January 1, 1897*
(With All Dividends Reinvested)

YEAR	VALUE AT END OF YEAR
1897	$ 1.25
1900	1.98
1920	7.25
1940	35.90
1960	466.50
1980	1,682.86
1990	7,193.81
1991	8,933.83

Note that as the 1900 dollar lost value over time, the Dow, with all dividends reinvested, rose dramatically above the rate of the reduced worth of the dollar. The rise more than compensated for the loss in value of the 1900 dollar.

...the value of the Dow has always returned to the point where it had been...

Except for a brief period between 1920-1932, the value of the dollar has steadily declined. In contrast, when the Dow falls, the value of the Dow has always returned to the point where it had been and continued to rise above it later. However, both the shrinking dollar value and gain in the Dow Jones Industrial Average did take TIME.

◆ Value of the Dow Adjusted for Dollar Loss

The next chart demonstrates the results of trading $1 for units of the Dow on January 1, 1897, and adjusting the value of those units for the declining value of a 1900 dollar over a 95-year period. These results include all reinvested dividends.

(13-4)   *Actual Value of $1 Invested in the Dow From 1897 Through 1991*
*(With **All** Dividends Reinvested)*
Adjusted for the Loss in the Value of a 1900 Dollar

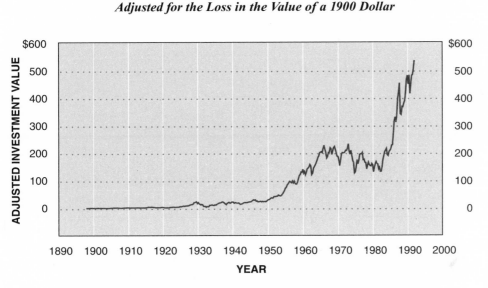

Source: *Investors Research Corporation based on data provided by Bureau of the Census and Bureau of Labor Statistics.*

A 1900 dollar invested in the Dow was worth $8,933.83 on December 31, 1991. If this result is adjusted for the loss in value, the chart above shows that the adjusted value would be $539.16, which is 539 times greater than a 1900 dollar. Obviously the increase in value of this hypothetical investment in the Dow more than compensated for the loss in value of a dollar.

This chart highlights the importance of trading a dollar for something that can maintain or exceed its original value.

TIME erodes the value of a dollar
but enhances the value of common stocks.

There are short-term
risks and long-term
opportunities...

Where Will the Dow Be in 10 Years?

No one can predict the future, but if a dollar were to lose one-half of its value in the next 10 years, the value of the Dow would have to double just to keep up with the loss in value of a dollar. If this happened, the Dow Jones Industrial Average would have to increase from 3,169 to over 6,338 by the end of the year 2001.

If you ever think that the value of the Dow may be too high, take time and ask yourself: Do you consider it **too high today**, when compared with where it has been in the past, or do you consider it too high when compared with where the Dow might be **in the future?**

Hypothetical Investments in the Dow

What are the short-term investment risks and the long-term investment opportunities of owning common stocks? To get a historical point of view, detailed studies were made of hypothetical investments in an unmanaged group of common stocks represented by the Dow Jones Industrial Average. This study covered various investment periods during the 95-year history of the Dow.

The purpose of this analysis was to identify the best and worst investment results for each selected period and to determine when these results occurred. Another objective was to identify where the middle 50% of the investment results occurred for each period.

Case I of this study assumes a **one-time investment of $10,000.**

Case II assumes **$100 is invested each month.**

In both cases, all dividends are reinvested.

The following assumptions were also made for both cases:

They encompassed 95 years beginning January 1897, and ending December 1991.

The money was invested in multiple "rolling" periods: one, three, five, 10, 15, 20, 25, and 30 years.

The starting point of the first investment period began on the first day of 1897 and lasted the duration of one of the multiple periods (one, three, five, 10, 15, 20, 25, and 30 years). The next investment period started at the beginning of the second quarter (April 1897) and also lasted the duration of one of the multiple periods. This process continued to advance one quarter of a year at a time until the last investment period ended on December 31, 1991.

There were 377 one-year investment periods during 95 years. The chart below illustrates how the one-year investment periods relate to each other.

The results of both cases demonstrate how an investment in the Dow fluctuates over various periods of time. They clearly illustrate the short-term risks and the long-term opportunities of such investments.

(13-5)   *One-Year Investment Periods*
                    Each Starting at the Beginning of a Quarter

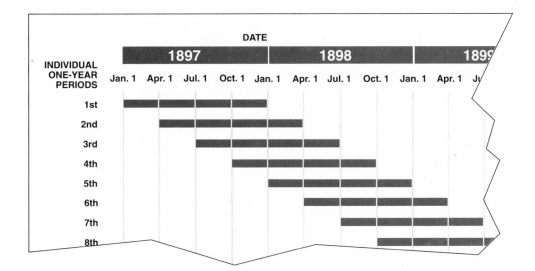

◆ Case I – One-Time Investment of $10,000

Case I follows an investment of $10,000 traded for units of the Dow. Remember, as long as it was held in those units, the investment was not tied to a dollar but instead was tied to the value of the Dow. At the beginning of each period considered, it was assumed a **one-time investment** was made on the first business day of that quarter. All dividends were reinvested immediately in additional units.

At the end of each individual period, the accumulated units of the Dow were traded back into dollars. Thus, each investment started with $10,000 and ended with a new dollar value. The difference between the starting and ending figures was converted to an **average annual percentage return**. The individual percentage returns were then listed in order, from the highest returns to the lowest.

Understanding the Case Study Charts

The easiest way to visualize and comprehend this information is through the use of simple charts. It is important that you take time to examine the individual elements in the charts. Try to understand and become comfortable with how **they were developed.*** This will help you interpret the results of the study.

Try to understand and become comfortable with the charts.

The elements are built up in Charts 13-6A through 13-6C to arrive at the final chart, 13-6D.

(13-6A)

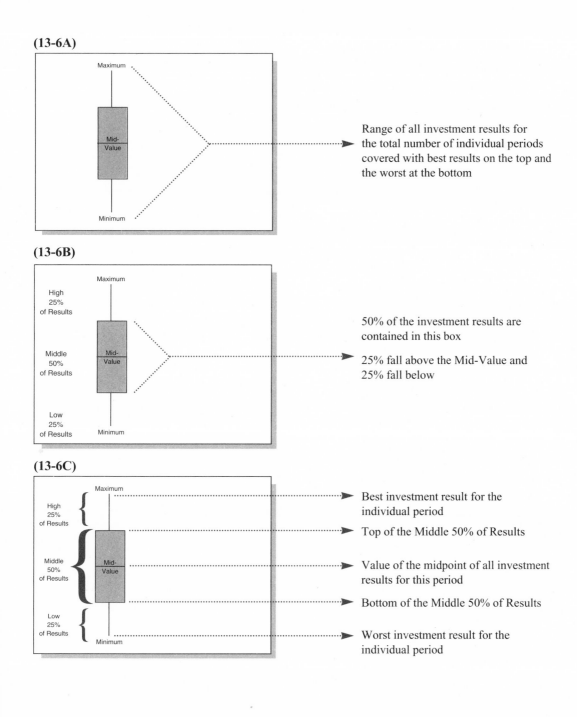

Range of all investment results for the total number of individual periods covered with best results on the top and the worst at the bottom

(13-6B)

50% of the investment results are contained in this box

25% fall above the Mid-Value and 25% fall below

(13-6C)

Best investment result for the individual period

Top of the Middle 50% of Results

Value of the midpoint of all investment results for this period

Bottom of the Middle 50% of Results

Worst investment result for the individual period

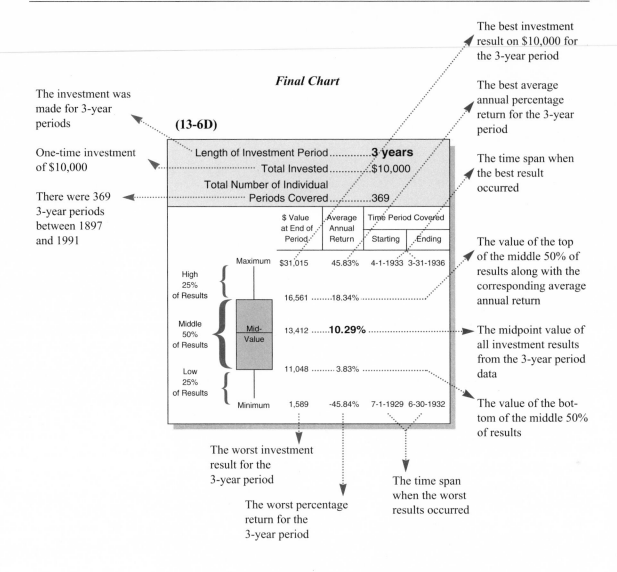

Final Chart

The investment was made for 3-year periods

One-time investment of $10,000

There were 369 3-year periods between 1897 and 1991

(13-6D)

The best investment result on $10,000 for the 3-year period

The best average annual percentage return for the 3-year period

The time span when the best result occurred

The value of the top of the middle 50% of results along with the corresponding average annual return

The midpoint value of all investment results from the 3-year period data

The value of the bottom of the middle 50% of results

The worst investment result for the 3-year period

The worst percentage return for the 3-year period

The time span when the worst results occurred

You may be as curious as I was to learn what the best and worst results were in each period and when they occurred. The following charts indicate the results for individual periods of time. Please note that these charts are **not** drawn to scale. Charts 13-7A and 13-7B summarize all of the eight individual periods (one, three, five, 10, 15, 20, 25, and 30 years).

(13-7A)

Amount of Investment........ $10,000 One Time
Investment in........ Dow Jones Industrial Average
(With All Distributions Reinvested)
Time Period Covered........ 1897 through 1991
(Progressing one quarter at a time)

Length of Investment Period............. **1 year**
Total Invested.............$10,000
Total Number of Individual
Periods Covered.............377

		$ Value at End of Period	Annual Return	Time Period Covered	
				Starting	Ending
High 25% of Results	Maximum	$23,813	138.13%	7-1-1932	6-30-1933
		12,718	27.18%		
Middle 50% of Results	Mid-Value	11,060	**10.60%**		
Low 25% of Results		9,658	-3.42%		
	Minimum	3,109	-68.91%	7-1-1931	6-30-1932

Length of Investment Period............. **3 years**
Total Invested.............$10,000
Total Number of Individual
Periods Covered.............369

		$ Value at End of Period	Average Annual Return	Time Period Covered	
				Starting	Ending
High 25% of Results	Maximum	$31,015	45.83%	4-1-1933	3-31-1936
		16,561	18.31%		
Middle 50% of Results	Mid-Value	13,412	**10.28%**		
Low 25% of Results		11,048	3.38%		
	Minimum	1,589	-45.84%	7-1-1929	6-30-1932

Length of Investment Period............. **5 years**
Total Invested.............$10,000
Total Number of Individual
Periods Covered.............361

		$ Value at End of Period	Average Annual Return	Time Period Covered	
				Starting	Ending
High 25% of Results	Maximum	$47,143	36.36%	7-1-1932	6-30-1937
		20,880	15.86%		
Middle 50% of Results	Mid-Value	16,353	**10.34%**		
Low 25% of Results		12,658	4.83%		
	Minimum	3,391	-19.45%	7-1-1927	6-30-1932

Length of Investment Period............. **10 years**
Total Invested.............$10,000
Total Number of Individual
Periods Covered.............341

		$ Value at End of Period	Average Annual Return	Time Period Covered	
				Starting	Ending
High 25% of Results	Maximum	$65,066	20.60%	7-1-1949	6-30-1959
		35,653	13.56%		
Middle 50% of Results	Mid-Value	24,175	**9.23%**		
Low 25% of Results		18,424	6.30%		
	Minimum	6,804	-3.78%	7-1-1929	6-30-1939

Not Drawn to Scale.

(13-7B)

		$ Value at End of Period	Average Annual Return	Time Period Covered	
				Starting	Ending
	Maximum	$146,367	19.59%	10-1-1914	9-28-1929
High 25% of Results		59,425	12.62%		
Middle 50% of Results	Mid-Value	37,246	**9.16%**		
Low 25% of Results		25,577	6.46%		
	Minimum	9,849	-0.10%	10-1-1929	9-30-1944

Length of Investment Period.............**15 years**
Total Invested.............$10,000
Total Number of Individual Periods Covered.............321

		$ Value at End of Period	Average Annual Return	Time Period Covered	
				Starting	Ending
	Maximum	$188,308	15.81%	4-1-1942	3-30-1962
High 25% of Results		95,803	11.96%		
Middle 50% of Results	Mid-Value	55,818	**8.98%**		
Low 25% of Results		38,975	7.04%		
	Minimum	14,563	1.90%	7-1-1929	6-30-1949

Length of Investment Period.............**20 years**
Total Invested.............$10,000
Total Number of Individual Periods Covered.............301

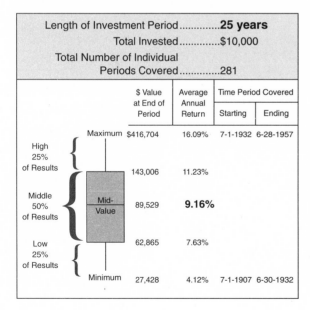

		$ Value at End of Period	Average Annual Return	Time Period Covered	
				Starting	Ending
	Maximum	$416,704	16.09%	7-1-1932	6-28-1957
High 25% of Results		143,006	11.23%		
Middle 50% of Results	Mid-Value	89,529	**9.16%**		
Low 25% of Results		62,865	7.63%		
	Minimum	27,428	4.12%	7-1-1907	6-30-1932

Length of Investment Period.............**25 years**
Total Invested.............$10,000
Total Number of Individual Periods Covered.............281

		$ Value at End of Period	Average Annual Return	Time Period Covered	
				Starting	Ending
	Maximum	$557,099	14.34%	7-1-1932	6-29-1962
High 25% of Results		209,078	10.66%		
Middle 50% of Results	Mid-Value	148,545	**9.41%**		
Low 25% of Results		112,772	8.41%		
	Minimum	41,411	4.85%	7-1-1902	6-30-1932

Length of Investment Period.............**30 years**
Total Invested.............$10,000
Total Number of Individual Periods Covered.............261

Not Drawn to Scale.

Compare the one-time $10,000 investment with the "$ Value at End of Period." See how these values change with the length of investment period.

Look at the one-year chart 13-7A. There was a wide variance in annual return results, with a total spread of over 207%, from 138% for the best one-year period to a minus 69% for the worst. It is interesting to note that the best one-year period was from July 1, 1932, to June 30, 1933, while the worst one-year period began one year earlier, July 1, 1931, and ended when the best results started, June 30, 1932.

An investment made on July 1, 1931 would have realized, one year later, the worst one-year result out of 377 periods (minus 69%). Most people, if they had experienced these poor results, would have assumed that this was an indication of future performance and would have become discouraged. Many would have traded their investment back for dollars and tried to find another place to invest their money. Had they had confidence in the long-term opportunities in the Dow and left their investment undisturbed for another 29 years (30 years total), it would have been worth $211,359. The original investment, which began with the worst one-year result, **grew at an average annual compound rate** of **10.7%** (one of the best 30-year results). As you can see, **it is unwise to assume that short-term investment results are an accurate indication of long-term performance**.

In the other charts, observe the best and worst "$ Value at End of Period." In each of the charts, pay special attention to the results of the **Middle 50% of Results**.

Observe that, in five out of the eight investment periods, the lowest result ended on June 30, 1932. Also notice that, in four of the eight periods, the best results started at the quarter beginning on July 1, 1932.

(13-8)   ***$10,000 Investments in the Dow Jones Industrial Average***
                              (With All Dividends Reinvested)

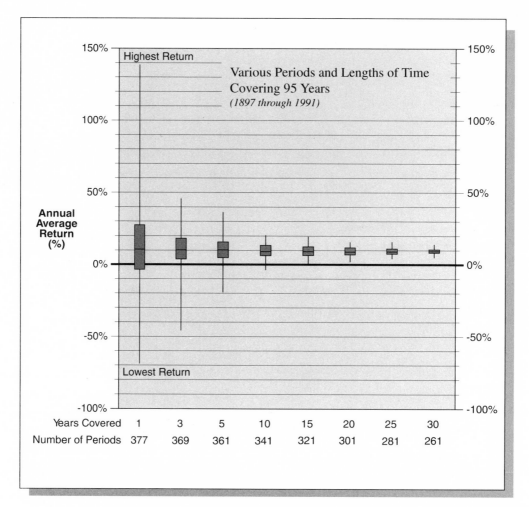

The chart above is drawn to scale. It presents the data from the preceding charts for comparative purposes. Beginning with the one-year period, the difference between the highest percentage return and the lowest return narrowed more rapidly the longer the investment was held. The spread in returns for the one-year period was 207%. This spread decreased for the 30-year period to only 9%. The 30-year results ranged from a high of 14% to a low of 5%, with the majority of results between 11% and 8%.

What, then, is the message? The longer an investment was held in the Dow, the less risk there was of suffering a loss. Starting with the 20-year period, there were **no losses at all**! Moreover, for each of the **Middle 50% of Results**, there were no losses starting with the three-year periods.

The table below illustrates the results of the study in a different way. This approach may appeal to those who think dealing in the stock market is like gambling, because it shows the probability of receiving a certain percentage return. It indicates the percentage of results which were in excess of various compound rates. It also indicates the total number of results within each period.

(13-9)   *The Probability of Receiving a Certain Return*
$10,000 Investments in the Dow Jones Industrial Average
(With All Dividends Reinvested)

Comparing Various Periods and Percentage Rates

Covering 95 Years (1897 through 1991)
*Percentage Results **in Excess of** Various Compound Rates*

PERIOD (YEARS)	0%	2%	4%	6%	8%	10%	12%	14%	16%	18%	20%	22%	24%	26%	28%	30%	NUMBER OF PERIODS
1	70	67	63	60	55	52	47	44	42	40	36	33	30	26	25	21	377
3	88	80	73	64	57	53	43	37	32	26	21	15	9	7	4	3	369
5	91	86	79	69	61	52	41	32	24	16	12	7	4	3	2	2	361
10	97	95	89	77	62	43	31	23	12	3	0	0	0	0	0	0	341
15	99	97	93	79	63	41	29	16	6	1	0	0	0	0	0	0	321
20	100	100	98	88	64	43	25	6	0	0	0	0	0	0	0	0	301
25	100	100	100	98	68	37	17	3	0	0	0	0	0	0	0	0	281
30	100	100	100	99	85	33	9	1	0	0	0	0	0	0	0	0	261

▲*
*There was only one 95-year investment period which had an average annual return of 10.04%

What was the probability of making money if you invested in the Dow for only one year? The chart indicates that there was a 70% chance of having a positive return. **The opportunity for a positive return**

increased the longer the investment was held. After 20 years, the chart indicates there was a 100% probability of earning a positive return.

Focus on the 6% column. Notice that the probability of receiving more than a 6% return increased from 60% for the one-year period to 99% for the 30-year period.

Look at the probability of receiving more than 14% over time. The probability rapidly **decreased** from 44% for the one-year period to 1% for the 30-year period.

If you are interested in learning what percentage of the 10-year period results received between an 8% and a 10% return, locate the probability percentages on the 10-year period line under the 8% and 10% columns and subtract one percentage figure from the other. For example in Table 13-9, if you subtract 43 from 62, you will find that 19% of the 10-year period results received an average of between 8% and 10%.

Overall, notice in Table 13-9 how the long-term probability results tend to "funnel" toward a 10% return in the 30-year period.

◆ Case II – An Investment of $100 a Month

You have seen the results of a one-time $10,000 investment. Since this amount might seem beyond your reach, it might be easier for you to relate to a $100-a-month investment. If this is the case, you might be curious to learn what were the best and worst results over various periods of time and when they occurred. Also, you might be interested in learning what the probabilities were of receiving a certain return and what was the effect of time on this regular investment.

Case II follows an investment of $100 a month with all dividends reinvested. The same assumptions of Case I are applicable to this segment.

While there is much that one can learn from these charts, let me highlight two key observations.

In the following $100-a-month investment charts:

1. **Every one** of the lowest results happened to end on the same date: June 30, 1932.

(13-10A)   *Amount of Investment.........$100 a Month*
                        Investment in.........Dow Jones Industrial Average
                  (With All Distributions Reinvested)
                  Time Period Covered.........1897 through 1991
                  (Progressing one quarter at a time)

Length of Investment Period.............**1 year**
Total Invested.............$1,200
Total Number of Individual Periods Covered.............377

	$ Value at End of Period	Annual Return	Time Period Covered	
			Starting	Ending
Maximum	$2,107	163.33%	7-1-1932	6-30-1933
High 25% of Results	1,406	33.14%		
Middle 50% of Results (Mid-Value)	1,306	**16.70%**		
Low 25% of Results	1,216	2.47%		
Minimum	739	-61.93%	7-1-1931	6-30-1932

Length of Investment Period.............**3 years**
Total Invested.............$3,600
Total Number of Individual Periods Covered.............369

	$ Value at End of Period	Average Annual Return	Time Period Covered	
			Starting	Ending
Maximum	$6,544	42.90%	1-2-1926	12-31-1928
High 25% of Results	4,807	19.69%		
Middle 50% of Results (Mid-Value)	4,293	**11.76%**		
Low 25% of Results	3,837	4.18%		
Minimum	1,280	-56.42%	7-1-1929	6-30-1932

Length of Investment Period.............**5 years**
Total Invested.............$6,000
Total Number of Individual Periods Covered.............361

	$ Value at End of Period	Average Annual Return	Time Period Covered	
			Starting	Ending
Maximum	$14,163	35.17%	1-2-1924	12-31-1928
High 25% of Results	9,195	17.09%		
Middle 50% of Results (Mid-Value)	7,882	**10.85%**		
Low 25% of Results	6,896	5.50%		
Minimum	1,863	-44.92%	7-1-1927	6-30-1932

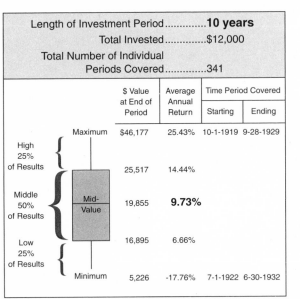

Length of Investment Period.............**10 years**
Total Invested.............$12,000
Total Number of Individual Periods Covered.............341

	$ Value at End of Period	Average Annual Return	Time Period Covered	
			Starting	Ending
Maximum	$46,177	25.43%	10-1-1919	9-28-1929
High 25% of Results	25,517	14.44%		
Middle 50% of Results (Mid-Value)	19,855	**9.73%**		
Low 25% of Results	16,895	6.66%		
Minimum	5,226	-17.76%	7-1-1922	6-30-1932

Not Drawn to Scale.

(13-10B)

		$ Value at End of Period	Average Annual Return	Time Period Covered	
				Starting	Ending
	Maximum	$95,165	19.95%	7-1-1914	6-29-1929
High 25% of Results		55,357	13.76%		
Middle 50% of Results	Mid-Value	39,074	**9.67%**		
Low 25% of Results		30,133	6.54%		
	Minimum	11,252	-6.57%	7-2-1917	6-30-1932

Length of Investment Period.............**15 years**
Total Invested.............$18,000
Total Number of Individual Periods Covered.............321

		$ Value at End of Period	Average Annual Return	Time Period Covered	
				Starting	Ending
	Maximum	$178,490	17.39%	10-1-1909	9-28-1929
High 25% of Results		101,327	12.80%		
Middle 50% of Results	Mid-Value	66,523	**9.28%**		
Low 25% of Results		50,903	6.98%		
	Minimum	21,331	-1.19%	7-1-1912	6-30-1932

Length of Investment Period.............**20 years**
Total Invested.............$24,000
Total Number of Individual Periods Covered.............301

		$ Value at End of Period	Average Annual Return	Time Period Covered	
				Starting	Ending
	Maximum	$287,569	15.26%	10-1-1904	9-28-1929
High 25% of Results		177,474	12.26%		
Middle 50% of Results	Mid-Value	118,043	**9.67%**		
Low 25% of Results		83,193	7.37%		
	Minimum	36,047	1.43%	7-1-1907	6-30-1932

Length of Investment Period.............**25 years**
Total Invested.............$30,000
Total Number of Individual Periods Covered.............281

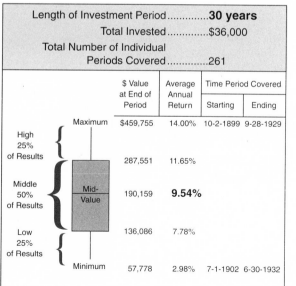

		$ Value at End of Period	Average Annual Return	Time Period Covered	
				Starting	Ending
	Maximum	$459,755	14.00%	10-2-1899	9-28-1929
High 25% of Results		287,551	11.65%		
Middle 50% of Results	Mid-Value	190,159	**9.54%**		
Low 25% of Results		136,086	7.78%		
	Minimum	57,778	2.98%	7-1-1902	6-30-1932

Length of Investment Period.............**30 years**
Total Invested.............$36,000
Total Number of Individual Periods Covered.............261

Not Drawn to Scale.

2. If each of these eight investments had been held just one more year, with no further investment and not traded back into dollars, they would have all gained 138% or increased 2.38 times, because the best "one-year" investment period result began on the next day, July 1, 1932 (see one-year investment period in Chart 13-7A).

(13-11)   *$100 a Month Invested in the Dow Jones Industrial Average*

(With All Dividends Reinvested)

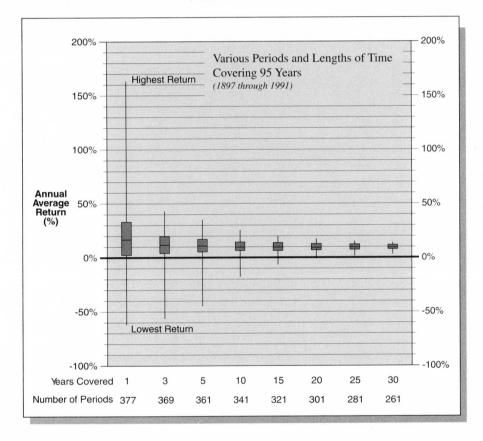

The data from the preceding charts is drawn to scale for comparative purposes in the chart above. You can also compare the differences and similarities to the $10,000 charts in Chart 13-8.

(13-12)   *The Probability of Receiving a Certain Return*

$100-a-Month Investments in the Dow Jones Industrial Average

(With All Dividends Reinvested)

Comparing Various Periods and Percentage Rates

Covering 95 Years (1897 through 1991)
Percentage Results in Excess of Various Compound Rates

PERIOD (YEARS)	0%	2%	4%	6%	8%	10%	12%	14%	16%	18%	20%	22%	24%	26%	28%	30%	NUMBER OF PERIODS
1	78	76	73	70	67	63	60	55	51	48	44	41	36	34	32	28	377
3	85	81	76	67	62	55	49	43	37	31	24	21	16	13	11	8	369
5	90	86	80	73	62	55	43	34	29	23	17	10	7	5	3	2	361
10	96	94	90	77	64	48	36	27	17	10	4	1	1	0	0	0	341
15	99	97	93	79	63	46	34	22	12	2	0	0	0	0	0	0	321
20	100	99	97	85	65	46	32	16	2	0	0	0	0	0	0	0	301
25	100	100	99	93	66	48	27	8	0	0	0	0	0	0	0	0	281
30	100	100	100	98	70	43	20	0	0	0	0	0	0	0	0	0	261

The table above shows the probability of receiving a certain rate of return while investing $100 a month. Compare these probabilities with those of a $10,000 investment shown in Table 13-9. If you study the similar periods and percentage rates of these charts, you will see that **the probability of receiving a higher percentage rate over time is generally slightly greater with periodic investments, in this case $100 a month**.

Summary

Here are some of the conclusions you can draw from these case studies of the Dow. **Even though there was no professional investment management, the long-term gains were impressive.**

There **were** short-term risks.

It is unwise to assume that short-term investment results are always a true indication of long-term performance.

There were long-term opportunities available if the investment was left alone.

Many people believe that investing is a form of gambling. In a way, this may appear to be true in the short term. The probabilities for profit on the investment significantly increased by lengthening the time the investment was held.

The importance of TIME cannot be overemphasized.

No one knows what will actually happen in the future, but the past **is** certainly an indication of what could happen.

Some questions to ask yourself:

If you had traded your money for an investment in the Dow and left it undisturbed for years, would you have been satisfied with the long-term results?

Is an investment kept in the Dow for more than three years not as much of a gamble as you once thought?

Do you believe this investment in common stocks keeps pace with and stays ahead of the loss in value of a dollar?

Do you believe this is a safe place to put your money over time?

Do you believe you would feel comfortable investing in the Dow over a long period of time?

Do you realize the probability of receiving a higher percentage rate is generally a little greater with a $100 a month than with a one-time investment?

Do you think you could expect better results having professionals manage your money?

There are short-term risks.

The purpose of an investment company
is to manage money professionally.

Managed Investments – Investment Companies

"I have never owned any marketable equity securities other than shares of mutual funds."

In 1924, bankers in New England introduced the investment company concept to America. For many years, these companies were not generally accepted by the investing public because of abuses in their operations and the absence of effective regulations. However, the Investment Company Act of 1940 provided safety measures which helped erase doubts about this type of investment.

After World War II, the full potential of the investment company concept began to be realized. This was due not only to restored public confidence, but also to a long rising market trend and the growing interest of people who had dollars to invest.

The purpose of an investment company is to manage money professionally. It provides a place where investors can pool their money, employ full-time professionals and pursue the goal of earning money with their money. The investment company belongs to the shareholders, not to management. It provides all the advantages usually available only to large investors.

Types of Investment Companies

There are two basic types of investment companies, **closed-end** and **open-end**. A closed-end company sells its shares to you but does not agree to buy back those shares in the future. If you buy shares of a closed-end investment company and want to sell them, you must find a buyer either in the over-the-counter market or on the stock exchange if the shares are traded there. Shares of closed-end investment companies often trade at a price below their asset value.

An open-end investment company is usually called a **mutual fund**. It not only sells shares to you but **also agrees to buy the shares back** at whatever their value might be in the future.

Investment companies are further categorized as **diversified** and **non-diversified**. With respect to 75% of the total value of the assets, a diversified company may invest no more than 5% in the securities of any one company or acquire more than 10% of the outstanding voting securities of a company. In addition, the typical diversified fund also follows a policy which prohibits the investment of more than 25% of its assets in any one industry. These requirements force diversification among various investments.

A non-diversified company is simply one that is not diversified. Of the two, the diversified investment company is the more popular.

All investment companies charge for professional management and shareholder services.

The **most** popular open-end companies, **mutual funds**, are further categorized as **load funds** or **no-load funds**.

Load Versus No-Load Funds

Load funds have a **sales charge** when you buy shares or when you sell (deferred sales charges) or both. These funds are usually distributed through brokers. These sales charges are over and above the investment management and shareholder servicing costs. Sales charges are used to pay commissions to brokers.

No-load funds **have no sales charge**, although there are still investment management and shareholder servicing costs which are paid for by the mutual fund itself.

Some funds, load or no-load, also have an annual charge for marketing expenses (12b-1 charges) shared by all fund shareholders because the fund pays these expenses directly.

Investment Objectives

Each mutual fund has a specific investment objective with clearly stated investment policies and restrictions. Some are imposed by the founders of the fund and some are imposed by law. Changes in a fund's investment objective or those investment policies or restrictions which are considered fundamental must be approved by its shareholders.

The investment objectives, restrictions, policies and all costs of a fund are described in great detail in a fact book called a **prospectus**, which is required to be made available by all funds. This document should be read carefully before purchasing fund shares to ensure that a fund's investment objectives coincide with yours.

◆ Policies that Differentiate Mutual Funds

Funds with the fewest restrictions allow the investment managers broad authority to use their best judgment to determine:

What to invest in.

Where to invest.

How much to invest.

How long to invest.

How much cash to hold if attractive investments cannot be found.

I would describe a fund that gives this broad authority to an investment manager as a **fully-managed fund**, since minimal limitations are

A shareholder … can relax and rely on the best judgment of the fund manager.

placed on management. Because of this broad authority, a shareholder having confidence in such a fund can relax and rely on the best judgment of the fund manager.

Funds with more restrictive policies **limit the investment manager** in the exercise of his best judgment when choosing investments that best match the fund's objective. For example, if a fund is prohibited from making investments in certain industries or is restricted to investing in one geographic area, the investment manager's best judgment is limited. In this case, the shareholder must be constantly alert and continue to make decisions about when to invest and when to redeem.

Some Attributes of Mutual Funds

I mentioned earlier the attributes of "ideal" investments. Now, let's relate these to mutual funds.

◆ Professional Management

Professional money management has long been available to large institutions and wealthy investors. Mutual funds make this kind of financial expertise available to everyone.

Mutual funds make professional money management available to everyone.

I believe that **professional management is the most important contribution to investment success over time**. The qualities of professional management described here are taken from my personal experience over the past 34 years since founding Twentieth Century Mutual Funds.

First and foremost, mutual fund managers are full-time professionals dedicated to managing the money invested in their funds. They bring to this trusted responsibility a specialized team of researchers, analysts, and state-of-the-art technology to ensure that the money invested, no matter what the amount, is given full-time attention. They invest, reinvest and seek the best opportunities for the assets they manage.

Admittedly, professional managers are not infallible. They may err in judgment and losses may occur on their selections. But usually **full-time, thoroughly trained managers and their support systems can do a better job than most individuals. Also, the results of their effort can be judged by their performance over time**.

◆ Diversification

Spreading investments over a number of different companies is advantageous, since some companies may lose value while others prosper. Mutual funds offer **instant diversification** on any amount of money. One share of a mutual fund represents part-ownership in a portfolio that holds many companies. Furthermore, diversification spreads risk not only over many companies, but also over many industries. Before mutual funds, diversification was a privilege largely available only to the wealthy who could diversify and purchase many securities.

Before mutual funds, diversification was a privilege largely available only to the wealthy who could diversify and purchase many securities.

For a mutual fund
investor, liquidity is
very important.

◆ Liquidity

For a mutual fund investor, liquidity is very important. Open-end mutual funds agree to redeem their shares each market day at their closing prices, usually called "net asset value." Shareholders can withdraw part or all of their investment at any time.

◆ Opportunity for Growth

Many investments are made with the hope of gain or growth. While there is no guarantee, judging by the past, common stock mutual funds certainly offer an opportunity for capital growth, particularly over the long term.

◆ Record Keeping

An important feature of mutual funds is that they are able to provide a complete record of your transactions.

When you own a share of a mutual fund, you are not required to keep records of the holdings represented by your ownership interest. The mutual fund does it for you. If you owned shares of all the companies owned by the fund, you would have to keep individual records for each company, which would certainly be a burdensome job.

◆ Availability in Convenient Amounts

Many investment options require a large initial investment, which closes the door to small investors. Most mutual funds, however, offer investment plans that allow investors to begin with a modest amount and add additional amounts periodically.

◆ Reinvestment Opportunity

In most mutual funds, income and capital gains distributions can be automatically reinvested. More than a convenience, this is a sound investment concept.

◆ Acceptability as Collateral

Normally, mutual fund investments are good collateral for a loan. Many types of investments may not be acceptable, either because the

Many investment options require a large initial investment, which closes the door to small investors.

bank is not familiar with the investment, the investment does not have sufficient liquidity, or the current value is not readily available. However, mutual funds are usually acceptable because they may be redeemed on demand and because they publish their value daily.

...common stock mutual funds may offer investors a reasonable inflation hedge over time, because the investment is not tied to the sinking value of a dollar...

◆ Current Information

Many investments provide little information after the original purchase is made, and the investor can only speculate as to the financial condition of the investment. A mutual fund, by law, must issue financial reports at regular intervals, disclosing full details regarding its holdings and its present condition. Current information is not only desirable, it should be insisted upon with any investment.

◆ Ease of Transfer

Mutual funds are often bought because their ownership is easily transferred from one person to another, unlike many other investment alternatives.

◆ Income Production

Mutual funds vary in the income they produce, depending on their investment objectives, but all funds pay an annual distribution of profits, when earned, and a distribution of any net income received from companies held in the portfolio. Some mutual funds maintain an objective of investing in common stocks that pay little or no dividends. These funds attempt to invest in companies that appreciate in value, rather than generate taxable dividends. Some funds offer "**check-a-month**" plans that provide monthly payments to you from your investment.

◆ Inflation Hedge

Owning shares in a common stock mutual fund whose objective is capital growth may offer investors a reasonable inflation hedge over time, because the investment is not tied to the sinking value of a dollar but to the value of growing companies.

(14-1)   *How Investments Compare Against "Ideal" Attributes Over Time*

Requisites of an Ideal Attribute Over Time	Stock Mutual Fund	Individual Common Stock	Fixed Income Mutual Fund	Individual Debt Security	Individual Real Estate	Fixed Insurance Annuity	Gold in Bars	Savings Account	Mortgage	Certificate of Deposit
Diversification	Yes	No	Yes	No	No	No	No	No	No	No
Record Keeping	Yes	No	Yes	No	No	No	No	Yes	Yes	Yes
Reinvestment Opportunities	Yes	Maybe	Yes	Maybe	No	No	No	Yes	No	Yes
Current Information	Yes	Yes	Yes	Yes	No	Maybe	Yes	Yes	Yes	Yes
Professional Management	Yes	No	Yes	No	No	Yes	No	Yes	No	Yes
Ease of Transfer	Yes	Yes	Yes	Yes	Maybe	Maybe	Yes	Yes	Maybe	Yes
Opportunity for Growth	Yes	Yes	Maybe	Maybe	Yes	No	Yes	No	No	No
Liquidity	Yes	Yes	Yes	Yes	No	Maybe	Maybe	Yes	No	Maybe
Available in Convenient Denominations	Yes	Yes	Yes	No	No	Yes	No	Yes	No	Yes
Inflation Hedge	Yes	Yes	No	No	Maybe	No	Yes	No	No	No
Income-Producing	Maybe	Maybe	Yes	Yes	Maybe	Yes	No	Yes	Yes	Yes
Acceptable as Collateral	Yes	Yes	Yes	Yes	Yes	Yes	Yes	Yes	Maybe	Yes
Limited Liability	Yes	Yes	Yes	Yes	Yes	Yes	Yes	Yes	Yes	Yes

The table above compares the attributes of an "ideal" investment with various types of investments.

My Beliefs About Mutual Funds

My Beliefs About Mutual Funds

All mutual funds are not equal –
some are better than others.

There are over 3,000 mutual funds. But just because an investment company is called a mutual fund and meets the criteria of an ideal investment doesn't necessarily mean that it's a good fund in which to invest.

A combination of investment objectives, restrictions, performance, ethics, qualifications of the managers, dedication and support systems contribute dramatically to the differences among mutual funds. In theory, all mutual funds have access to the entire common stock and fixed income market, but not all are solid performers over time.

Many funds state similar investment objectives. In fact, many have the same investment philosophy, but very few have outstanding and consistent results over time.

It is important that you understand the investment philosophy, objectives and policies of any mutual fund in which you invest. Is the philosophy logical? Does it make sense? How does the fund intend to implement its investment philosophy? Does it follow its discipline consistently year after year, or does it change its approach frequently?

Most importantly, examine the investment results of the fund. What is the record of the investment manager? Has the fund been successful over time? Are the results consistent? How do the results compare with those funds with similar objectives?

Equity Investments Over Time

I believe the soundest place to have your investment assets over time is in a common stock mutual fund that has ownership interest in a group of the most successful companies.

Why do I believe this?

♦ Successful companies have proven that they offer a unique, outstanding product or service which creates a strong demand.

♦ Such companies have demonstrated that they have the ability to sustain and increase profits by adjusting costs and even raising prices, thus compensating for the shrinking value of a dollar.

♦ Rising profits increase the demand for the companies' shares, keeping their market value higher than other less successful companies. **The greater the demand for shares,** the higher the market value.

By owning an interest in a group of **successful companies** through a mutual fund, you have a real opportunity to stay ahead of the shrinking value of a dollar and to accumulate wealth.

A successful company is one whose earnings and revenues are growing at an "accelerating rate." Identifying such companies requires computer technology and the techniques of a sophisticated on-line data processing system – resources available to a good fund manager.

When the train leaves the station, you need to be on it.

In addition, I strongly believe that the more successful investment managers **remain "fully invested," instead of speculating with your money** by attempting to predict how much should be kept in cash while trying to predict which direction the market will go. If the investment manager remains fully invested, the fund is able to catch the upward spurts I described earlier. In other words, when the train leaves the station you need to be on it.

After decades of experience, it is my opinion that it is best to invest in companies paying little or no dividends. **Dividends are not as important as earnings. Earnings must come first**. A company must earn money before it should pay any dividends. However, before dividends can be paid to shareholders, taxes must be paid by the company on its earnings. If dividends are paid out by a company, they are in effect taxed twice because a tax is incurred first by the company and second by the shareholder. But if the earnings are kept by the company and not paid out in dividends, the money is taxed only once. In this case, the retained earnings can be put to work to generate more earnings, which in turn can further increase the value of the company. As the market value of companies in a specific fund increases, so does the value of the fund.

My $10,000 Invested in "Fund A"

In 1958, I was one of the founders of Twentieth Century Investors, Inc. The company initially offered just two mutual funds. The purpose of this book is not to sell a specific mutual fund but to make you aware that you can achieve financial independence. For this reason, I will not mention one of the funds by name but refer to it as Fund A.

Before the fund could be offered to the public, it had to raise at least $100,000 of capital. To show my confidence and belief in the endeavor, I personally traded $10,000 for shares of Fund A.

*I still own those shares today. From October 31, 1958 to December 31, 1991, my investment grew at an average rate of 15.6% a year. During that time there have been wars, severe inflation, recessions, and the famous October 1987 "correction." The value of my $10,000 investment has not grown at a constant rate over time; I did not expect that it would. In fact, it has fluctuated widely in price. However, **if** I had wanted to trade my investment back into dollars, I could have exchanged those shares for $1,218,215 on December 31, 1991.*

*When people hear of results such as these, they believe I was "lucky." They don't believe they could achieve such results themselves over time with similar investments. But who is to say they could not? Years ago, I was **absolutely** determined to achieve financial independence. I made my original investment of $10,000 and then remained patient, allowing time to work for me. No miracles were expected; I simply had the confidence in a fully-managed investment and believed in the power of compounding over time.*

From October 31, 1958 through December 31, 1991, the dollar lost 80% of its value at an average rate of 4.6% a year. Because of this, I could have traded my shares of Fund A for many more dollars in 1991 because the dollars were worth about one-fifth as much as they were in 1958. While I could have exchanged my shares for $1,218,215 on December 31, 1991, it should be understood that these 1991 dollars would actually buy only what $243,643 would have bought in 1958 (100% - 80% = 20% x $1,218,215 = $243,643). This bit of reality further underscores the importance of a growing investment that beats the continued shrinking value of a dollar.

I remained patient, allowing time to work for me.

Fixed Income Investments

When it comes to fixed income investments, my experience has shown that people are more interested in receiving the return OF their money than receiving a return ON their money.

In direct contrast to common stocks, which I consider to be long-term investments, fixed income securities are worthwhile investments for the short term.

This short-term limited risk is due to the nature of these investments. When you buy fixed income securities (bonds, for example), you are **lending** money to a company or to the government in exchange for interest payments.

Unlike common stocks, these "debt" securities do not represent ownership interests in a company; their value does not increase as the company's value increases, so long as interest rates remain unchanged. Because debt securities are tied to a dollar, they cannot protect your investment against the dollar's declining value over time.

A Potential Financial Risk

Financial institutions offering fixed income investments to the public are in competition with each other to attract dollars. The more money they can accumulate under their own management, the greater their profits. If the highest interest rate attracts the most money, many institutions will strive to provide the highest rate.

Within a specific investment sector, there is only a limited supply of quality investments available from which all institutions may choose. All investments of the same quality in a particular sector generally provide the same amount of yield or interest. So, if an institution wants to increase the yield on one of its products, it must increase the risk and buy lower quality investments. The competition to have the highest yield is so great that lower quality investments are sometimes used to gain a higher yield and, in so doing, the degree of risk is greatly increased.

Financial institutions …are in competition with each other to attract dollars.

I believe most people are interested in receiving the highest yield possible, *but only from quality investments*. I do not believe people want to assume increased risk by owning lower-quality investments.

… periodic investing
enhances your
opportunity for
making a profit
over time.

The Amazing Results of Regular Investments

*When share prices vary up and down, periodic investing
enhances your opportunity for making a profit over time.*

You might think that since a certain fund did well in the past, it will do well in the future. But no one knows for certain. Even if you are optimistic and believe you will make a reasonable return on your investment, you still have the nagging question: What does the future offer?

Simply stated, only one of three things can happen to your investment. Your future results can only be:

> Identical to the past
> Better than the past
> Worse than the past

What Does the Future Offer?

Perhaps this question can be answered by studying the two hypothetical investments in Chart 16-1 – Investment **"A"** and Investment **"B."** Let's assume that for each investment, you make two decisions:

1. You intend to invest $100 every month without fail

   and

2. You intend to do this for 10 years.

What does the future offer?

Obviously, the price per share of your investments could go either up or down. Chart 16-1 shows that in Investment **A** the price continually goes up, while in Investment **B** the price initially goes down, then later returns only to its starting point. These are deliberately exaggerated examples to illustrate a key concept about regular investing. They do not refer to a specific investment. Taxes have not been considered since they would only cloud the message.

First, with **A,** your investment starts at $6 a share and the price continues to increase every month, year after year, reaching $16 a share at the end of the tenth year. The price always goes up, never down in value. Under Investment **A,** you pay a slightly higher amount for a share each time you invest.

Second, in **B,** your investment starts at $6 a share, the same as **A,** but the price per share goes **down** for the first five years, to a low of $1.50 per share. Then, over the last five years, the price returns **only** to the **original price** of $6 a share. In other words, in **B,** the price continues to drop every month for the first five years, then increases for the last five years. The price per share starts at $6 a share and, after 10 long years, ends at only $6 a share. It is never higher.

(16-1)   *Share Prices for A and B*

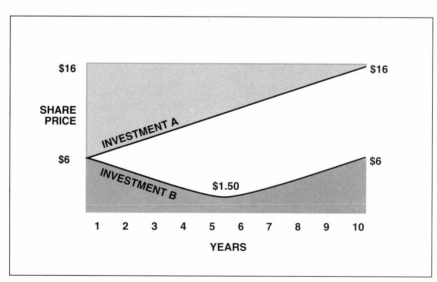

Assume you follow through with both of your intentions of (1) investing each and every month and (2) investing continuously for the full 10 years. Of these two investments, **A** and **B,** which would offer you the greatest opportunity for profit? Would the value of your investment be greater by following to completion **A** or **B** ? If you selected **A,** the obvious choice, you would have made money. But, as hard as it may be to believe, you would have done better if you had you followed Investment **B.**

Here is why. In either investment, you would have invested $100 each month, month after month, for 10 years. Therefore, you would have invested $1,200 each year or $12,000 in 10 years. At the end of 10 years, **A** would have been worth $18,919, while **B** would have been worth $24,130. Investment **B** would have been 40% more profitable than **A.**

Most people would naturally choose **A,** because they think the share price **must** go up regularly in order to make a profit. In **B,** the price did not always go up; rather, it went down for the first five years, providing the opportunity for **buying many more shares with your money**. Even though at maturity the price of each share in Investment **B** never exceeded the original price of $6 a share, at the end of 10 years **B** was the better investment. This is not magic. When the price of your shares was low, each of your $100 investments bought more shares. In fact during the 10 years, you accumulated over three times as many shares as in **A.**

…the price of your shares does not necessarily have to go up each month in order for you to have a profit.

Is there any probability of Investment **A** or **B** actually occurring? Probably not. Investing experience shows that reality is usually somewhere in between. The important point is that if you consistently invest at planned intervals over a sustained period of time, the price of your shares does not necessarily have to go up each month in order for you to have a profit. Certainly, if you were forced to liquidate your investment at a time when your shares were worth less than you paid for them, you would have a loss.

Again, the key message here is: **When share prices vary, periodic investing enhances your opportunity for making a reasonable profit over time**.

◆ What Happens in Between?

To continue this example, the results of Investments **A** and **B** could be seriously affected if they were terminated before 10 years. For example, selling any time in the first six years would assure a loss in **B** versus a smaller gain in Investment **A.**

(16-2)   *Results During 10-Year Period*

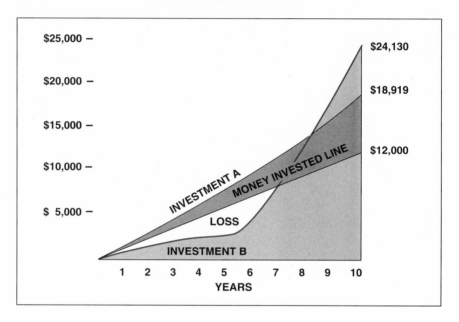

When you follow Investment **B** in the chart above, the line representing **B** is below the **Money Invested Line** for the first six years and eight months. Obviously, the greatest loss would have occurred at the end of the fifth year, when the price of the shares reached the lowest point. If you were forced to terminate your investment at this point, you would have suffered approximately a 50% loss. A short-term loss should not influence your thinking when you intend to invest over a long period, but it illustrates investment risks.

From the halfway point in this example, the line representing Investment **B** rapidly rises and crosses the **Money Invested Line** in less than two years from the low. If you were forced to terminate your investment at this point, you would realize a profit. Investment **B** continues to rise rapidly to become the more profitable investment at the end of 10 years. It is important for you to notice that for the first 97 months, the results of **A** would be greater than **B.** At the end of 10 years (120 months), however, Investment **B**, coming from behind, would be more profitable by a wide margin.

Again, these examples were based upon two assumptions:

1. You would have invested money each month, not missing a single month. **If you missed only one month, the results of both Investment A and B would be different.**

2. You were determined to invest your $100 a month for 10 years, not five years or eight years, but 10 years.

A short-term loss should not influence your thinking...

For simplicity, it was assumed there would be **no income** or earnings from either Investment **A** or **B**. Only the price per share varied up and down. If earnings or income had been considered and if they had been reinvested in additional shares each year, the results of both Investment **A** and **B** would have been greater at the end of 10 years.

◆ Another Possibility to Consider

Thus far, we have discussed the results of an investment of $100 a month for 10 years in Investment **A** and **B**. We also have reviewed what happens if you terminate either investment before completion. Now consider what would happen if you could no longer live up to your first goal – investing $100 each month – but you could achieve your other objective of leaving your money invested for the full 10 years.

Say you stopped investing at the end of the fifth year, when the price of your shares would be the lowest in Investment **B**. In this case, which plan would give you the greatest opportunity for profit at the end of 10 years – Investment **A** or **B** ?

During the first five years, you would have invested a total of $6,000 in both Investments **A** and **B**. Without any additional investment after the fifth year, the worth of the shares you accumulated during the first five years increased substantially during the second five-year period (16-3).

(16-3)   *Results if Forced to Discontinue Investing*

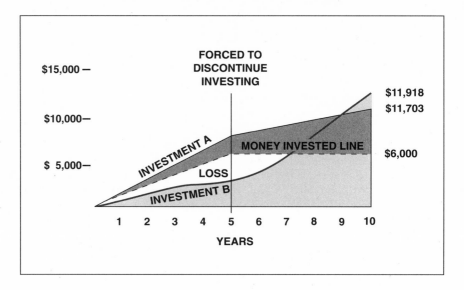

At the end of 10 years, the total worth of Investments **A** and **B** would be approximately the same. Investment **A** would be worth $11,703; **B** would be worth $11,918. Note that in this hypothetical example, using this **extreme case,** the worth of the investment at the end of 10 years is approximately two times the $6,000 originally invested.

You invested each month during the first five years a total of $6,000, then stopped. What happened to your investment?

Referring to Chart 16-3, the broken line is the **Money Invested Line** that represents your cost. This line increases for the first five years to $6,000 and then is level from the fifth year to the tenth year. You invested $100 a month for the first five years, then discontinued all investing from the fifth year on.

The line representing Investment **A is always above the Money Invested Line**, so that if you terminated your investment at any time, you would have realized a profit in this hypothetical example. If you had followed Investment **B** and terminated your investment before the seventh year, you would have suffered a loss. This loss would vary in size, depending upon when you were forced to sell. The greatest loss would occur at the end of the fifth year. Investment **B** becomes profitable after seven years, one month. The amount of the profit increases rapidly to the tenth year.

Why did Investment **B** do so well at the end of 10 years? It is simple. Again when the price of the shares was low, each of your $100 investments bought more shares. By the end of the fifth year, you would have accumulated over $2\frac{1}{2}$ times as many shares as in Investment **A. As the price of the shares increased, your potential loss rapidly changed to profit.**

We have taken two hypothetical examples, Investments **A** and **B,** and studied them from different investment perspectives. You obviously know you will make money in an investment if the price continues upward, as in Investment **A**. I hope these hypothetical examples have increased your understanding of the real probability of making money over time, even if the price fluctuates as it did in Investment **B**.

These illustrations show that you have an opportunity to become more financially secure if you follow through with a program of investing each month for a committed period of time.

The Benefits of a Managed Investment

The Benefits of a Managed Investment

*Professional investment management
can add real value.*

The examples in Chapter 13 show the results of an unmanaged hypothetical investment in the Dow Jones Industrial Average over varying periods of time covering a total of 95 years. Now let's compare the potential added value that professional management can offer.

For a managed investment, let us study the results of "Fund A" – one of the two mutual funds I founded in October 1958. Because the fund implemented its current investment discipline and practices on June 30, 1971, I will not go back beyond that date for this analysis.

First, a little information regarding the fund: This particular fund's investment objective is to seek capital growth by investing primarily in common stocks that are considered to have better than average prospects for appreciation. The fund's investment management team searches for successful companies whose earnings and revenues are believed to be growing at an accelerated rate. These companies are **not required** to pay dividends. The team is aided by the use of a unique and proprietary computer system developed in the early '70s to accelerate the process of identifying these companies. This system provides the investment management team with the opportunity to significantly improve the investment results.

The mutual fund's investment management team searches for successful companies whose earnings and revenues are believed to be growing...

157

The following guidelines have been used for this study:

It encompassed $20\frac{1}{2}$ years, from July 1, 1971, through December 31, 1991.

Multiple "rolling" periods are covered: one-, three-, five-, 10-, 15- and 20-year durations.

The starting point of the first investment period began the first day of July 1971 and lasted the duration of one of the multiple periods (one, three, five, 10, 15, 20 years). The next investment period started at the beginning of the second quarter (October 1971) and also lasted the duration of one of the multiple periods. This process continued to advance one quarter of a year at a time until the last investment period ended on December 31, 1991.

There were 79 one-year investment periods during $20\frac{1}{2}$ years. There were only three 20-year periods.

One-Time Investment of $10,000

In this segment, let's assume that $10,000 was traded for shares of Fund A, a fully-managed no-load (no sales charges) common stock mutual fund. At the beginning of each period considered, assume that a one-time investment was made on the first business day of that quarter. All dividends from investment income and distributions from realized profits were reinvested in additional shares.

At the end of each period, the accumulated shares of Fund A were traded back into dollars. Each investment started with $10,000 and each period ended with a certain dollar value. The difference between these two figures was converted to an average annual percentage return. The individual percentage returns were then listed in order of value from the highest to the lowest as in prior examples.

For comparison, two different **unmanaged** investments were made with the same amounts and over the same periods of time. One was a hypothetical investment in the Dow Jones Industrial Average. The other hypothetical investment was in the Standard & Poor's 500 Index (S&P 500). This latter index is an unmanaged group of 500 stocks, which many consider to be more representative of the stock market in general than the Dow Jones Industrial Average. No expenses or fees are reflected in either the Dow or the S&P 500 results. Management and service fees and brokerage expenses are, however, deducted from the fully-managed investment in Fund A, naturally reducing its results. No taxes are reflected in any of the investment results.

(17-1)   *$10,000 Investments in "Fund A"*

(With All Dividends Reinvested)

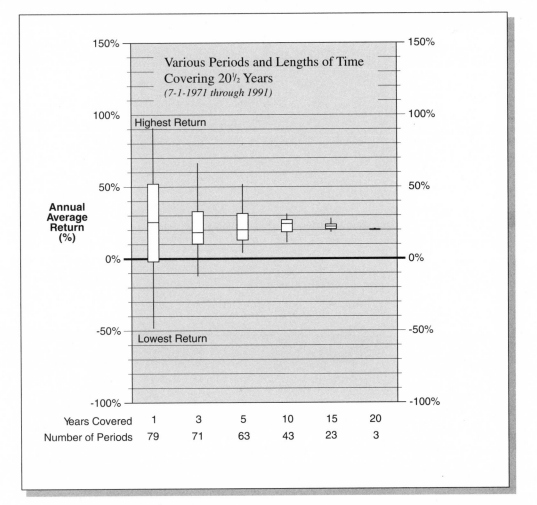

Various Periods and Lengths of Time Covering 20½ Years
(7-1-1971 through 1991)

The results are presented using two different methods. The first is illustrated with charts. The second uses tables that show the probability of receiving a certain percentage return. The original concept of the charts is fully explained in Chapter 13 (Charts 13-5, 13-6A, and 13-6B).

I have selected a small number of representative charts to help you understand the actual investment results of Fund A. (A complete set of charts for all three investments can be found in Addendum B.)

In Chart 17-1, the various periods of Fund A have been drawn to scale and can be compared with one another. Clearly, the extreme spread of percentage values from the highest return to the lowest return for each individual period narrowed rapidly from the one-year results through the 20-year results. The total percentage spread of one-year results was 139%, from a high of 91% to a low of minus 48%. By comparison, the 20-year total spread was much less, amounting to only 1%, with a high of 21% to a low of 20%.

The **Middle 50% of Results** for a one-year period fell between a high of 52% and a low of minus 2%, or a total spread of 54%. The spread for the **Middle 50% of Results** of the 15-year period was reduced to only 3%, with a high of 24% and a low of 21%.

Comparable charts of the Dow Jones and S&P 500 are found in Addendum B.

(17-2) *Comparing the Percentage Spreads of the Overall Results*

($10,000 Investments 7-1-1971 through 1991)

	One-Year Periods			20-Year Periods		
	Spread	*around*	Mid-Value	Spread	*around*	Mid-Value
"Fund A"	139%	*around*	25%	1.27%	*around*	20%
Dow	93%	*around*	12%	.50%	*around*	11%
S&P 500	101%	*around*	15%	.55%	*around*	12%

Table 17-2 compares the **percentage spreads** (the range from the highest return for any given period to the lowest return) of the overall results of Fund A (a fully-managed investment) to those of the Dow and S&P 500 (unmanaged investments). The total spreads are greater for Fund A than the other two, but you should note how much higher the Mid-Value is for Fund A when compared with the Mid-Value for the Dow and the S&P 500. In each case, the spread is around the Mid-Value.

The fully-managed fund in time pulled away from the two unmanaged investments.

Comparing Identical Period Charts

Addendum B contains the individual charts of the three different investments drawn to scale for each one of the separate five-year periods so they can be easily compared. (See Charts B10 through B15 for more information.)

The most significant of these charts, B15, is repeated as Chart 17-3 on page 162. Observe how the results of the fully-managed fund in time pulled away from the other two unmanaged investments. The lowest result of Fund A was higher than even the highest results of the other two.

(17-3)   *20-Year Results*

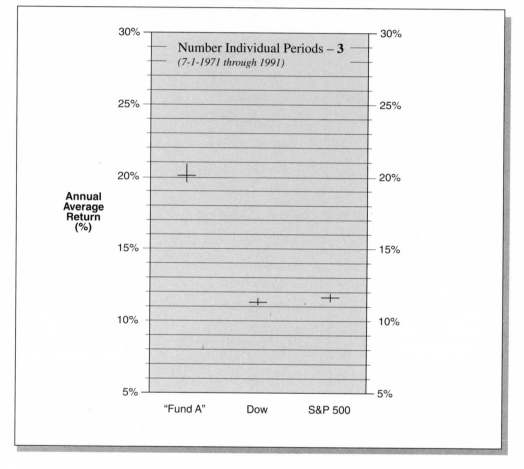

$10,000 One-Time Investment
(With All Dividends Reinvested)
Results of "Fund A" compared with the results of
Dow Jones Industrial Average and Standard & Poor's 500

The Mid-Value for Fund A was 20.09%, which was much higher than the other two. The Dow was 11.30%, and the S&P 500 was 11.65%. During this 20-year period, it is interesting to note that the dollar lost a total of 73% of its value at the annual rate of 6.3%.

(17-4A) *The Probabilities of Receiving a Certain Return*
$10,000 One-Time Investment
(With All Dividends Reinvested)

Comparing "Fund A" results with those of Dow Jones Industrial Average and Standard & Poor's 500

Covering 20½ Years (7-1-1971 through 1991)
*Percentage Results **in Excess of** Various Compound Rates*

"Fund A"

PERIOD (YEARS)	0%	2%	4%	6%	8%	10%	12%	14%	16%	18%	20%	22%	24%	26%	28%	30%	NUMBER OF PERIODS
1	71	71	67	67	67	65	63	61	61	58	57	54	53	49	46	46	79
3	90	89	86	86	82	76	69	66	61	51	49	45	38	35	34	31	71
5	100	100	100	97	94	87	81	71	63	59	51	43	40	37	29	27	63
10	100	100	100	100	100	100	100	98	91	84	67	56	51	35	19	5	43
15	100	100	100	100	100	100	100	100	100	100	87	61	22	9	4	0	23
20	100	100	100	100	100	100	100	100	100	(100)	67	0	0	0	0	0	3

Dow Jones Industrial Average

PERIOD (YEARS)	0%	2%	4%	6%	8%	10%	12%	14%	16%	18%	20%	22%	24%	26%	28%	30%	NUMBER OF PERIODS
1	70	68	65	61	57	54	49	46	43	42	37	34	30	25	24	22	79
3	90	83	79	72	66	58	52	45	38	30	20	7	6	4	4	4	71
5	100	97	83	75	65	62	59	48	32	22	17	10	5	5	5	2	63
10	100	100	95	84	81	70	58	47	26	9	0	0	0	0	0	0	43
15	100	100	100	100	100	91	61	13	4	0	0	0	0	0	0	0	23
20	100	100	100	100	100	(100)	0	0	0	0	0	0	0	0	0	0	3

Standard & Poor's 500

PERIOD (YEARS)	0%	2%	4%	6%	8%	10%	12%	14%	16%	18%	20%	22%	24%	26%	28%	30%	NUMBER OF PERIODS
1	75	70	68	67	62	58	56	53	47	43	34	29	28	25	24	20	79
3	90	87	86	79	70	62	54	48	41	27	14	7	6	6	3	1	71
5	98	95	89	83	76	70	63	57	32	16	10	5	5	5	2	0	63
10	100	100	100	93	84	79	70	53	33	2	0	0	0	0	0	0	43
15	100	100	100	100	100	96	65	30	9	0	0	0	0	0	0	0	23
20	100	100	100	100	100	(100)	0	0	0	0	0	0	0	0	0	0	3

(100) Represents the point at which the highest rate of return occurs for all the 20-year investment periods.

The table shown on the preceding page illustrates the same information in a different way, when a fully-managed investment is compared with the results of two unmanaged investments. Compare the probability of receiving greater than 0% interest with each investment. Also, compare what the probability was of receiving more than 6%. What were the chances of receiving more than 14%? Was the probability greater with the fully-managed investment?

Chart 17-4B, on the following page, was created by using the probability data from the 16% columns in Table 17-4A. This three-dimensional view helps you visualize how the probabilities of the three investments (Fund A, the Dow and the S&P 500) compare with each other over different periods of time. Note the dramatic differences between a fully-managed fund and unmanaged investments.

It is important to keep in mind that all of the results of Fund A have been relatively understated because each year a service cost, an investment management fee and trading commissions were deducted from the results. On the other hand, no expenses of any kind are reflected in the Dow or S&P 500 results. If applicable fees **had** been deducted from the Dow's and S&P 500's results, the difference in performance would have been even greater.

Professional investment
management can
lead to real value.

(17-4B) *The Probabilities of Receiving a 16% Return*
$10,000 One-Time Investment

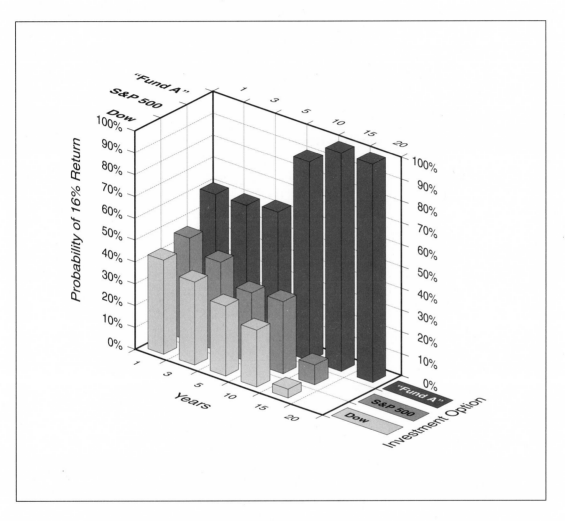

An Investment of $100 a Month

This segment covers an investment of $100 a month with all dividends reinvested in Fund A, the Dow and the S&P 500. The same assumptions stated for the one-time $10,000 investment apply to this segment.

I have selected certain charts on all three $100 investments to demonstrate the results of this study. A complete set for all three investments can be found in Addendum C.

Compare the differences and similarities in the chart below with the $10,000 investments shown in Chart 17-1.

(17-5)   *$100-a-Month Investments in "Fund A"*
                                        (With All Dividends Reinvested)

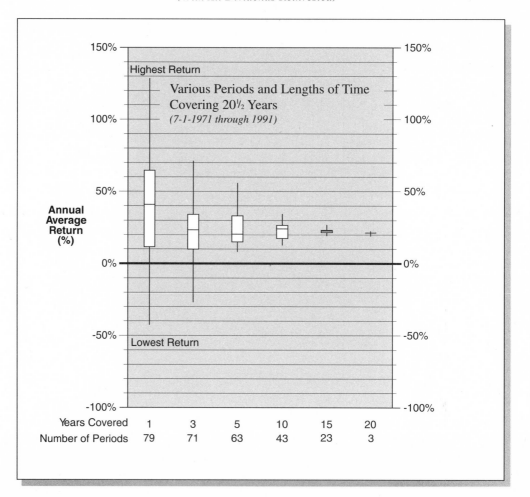

Compare the percentage spreads of the overall results in the $100-a-month investment in the chart below with the same information in the $10,000 investments in Chart 17-2.

(17-6) ***Comparing the Percentage Spreads of the Overall Results***

($100-a-Month Investments 7-1-1971 through 1991)

	One-Year Periods			20-Year Periods		
	Spread	*around*	**Mid-Value**	**Spread**	*around*	**Mid-Value**
"Fund A"	171%	*around*	41%	.83%	*around*	22%
Dow	109%	*around*	15%	.50%	*around*	14%
S&P 500	105%	*around*	14%	.73%	*around*	14%

Addendum C contains the individual charts of the three different investments drawn to scale for each of the separate periods so that they can be easily compared with one another. (See Charts C10 through C15 for more information.)

The most important of those charts (C15) is repeated on the next page as Chart 17-7. Again, notice that the investment results of the fully-managed Fund A are significantly higher than the best results of the other two unmanaged investments. There were only three "rolling" 20-year period results in the $20\frac{1}{2}$ years ending December 31, 1991. The Mid-Value of Fund A was 21.52% – a much higher rate than the other two unmanaged investments. The Dow was 13.87% and the S&P 500 was 14.07%. By way of comparison during this 20-year period, the dollar lost a total of 73% of its value at the rate of 6.3% a year.

(17-7)   *20-Year Results*
$100 a Month
(With All Dividends Reinvested)
Results of "Fund A" compared with the results of
Dow Jones Industrial Average and Standard & Poor's 500

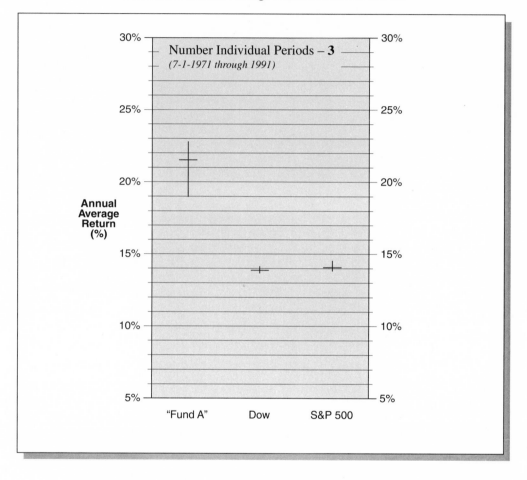

The table on the next page shows the same information regarding a $100-a-month investment. It illustrates the probability of receiving a certain return.

(17-8A) *The Probabilities of Receiving a Certain Return*
$100-a-Month Investment
(With All Dividends Reinvested)

Comparing "Fund A" results with those of Dow Jones Industrial Average and Standard & Poor's 500

Covering 20½ Years (7-1-1971 through 1991)
*Percentage Results **in Excess of** Various Compound Rates*

"Fund A"

PERIOD (YEARS)	0%	2%	4%	6%	8%	10%	12%	14%	16%	18%	20%	22%	24%	26%	28%	30%	NUMBER OF PERIODS
1	82	82	81	80	80	80	75	73	73	71	68	67	65	63	62	61	79
3	94	94	92	89	86	75	69	66	65	59	54	52	49	45	39	39	71
5	100	100	100	100	100	94	86	83	70	63	52	49	41	37	32	27	63
10	100	100	100	100	100	100	100	95	86	67	63	60	53	33	21	16	43
15	100	100	100	100	100	100	100	100	100	100	87	70	22	9	0	0	23
20	100	100	100	100	100	100	100	100	100	(100)	67	33	0	0	0	0	3

Dow Jones Industrial Average

PERIOD (YEARS)	0%	2%	4%	6%	8%	10%	12%	14%	16%	18%	20%	22%	24%	26%	28%	30%	NUMBER OF PERIODS
1	73	71	70	66	65	61	57	53	47	44	35	27	25	24	19	15	79
3	92	85	80	75	69	63	55	46	37	25	17	15	11	8	7	7	71
5	100	98	95	84	71	67	56	51	38	25	14	11	8	8	5	3	63
10	100	100	100	91	86	84	70	58	53	21	7	2	0	0	0	0	43
15	100	100	100	100	100	100	100	83	26	0	0	0	0	0	0	0	23
20	100	100	100	100	100	100	(100)	33	0	0	0	0	0	0	0	0	3

Standard & Poor's 500

PERIOD (YEARS)	0%	2%	4%	6%	8%	10%	12%	14%	16%	18%	20%	22%	24%	26%	28%	30%	NUMBER OF PERIODS
1	77	72	68	68	67	62	59	52	46	41	38	33	30	29	24	20	79
3	93	90	87	80	76	65	56	49	41	27	23	13	10	7	6	4	71
5	100	100	98	94	83	71	62	56	30	19	14	8	8	5	0	0	63
10	100	100	100	100	93	88	84	67	49	16	7	0	0	0	0	0	43
15	100	100	100	100	100	100	100	91	30	0	0	0	0	0	0	0	23
20	100	100	100	100	100	100	(100)	67	0	0	0	0	0	0	0	0	3

(100) Represents the point at which the highest rate of return occurs for all the 20-year investment periods.

Relate Table 17-8A on the preceding page to the probabilities of receiving a certain return on $10,000 one-time investments (Table 17-4A).

Again, it is interesting to observe that the probability of receiving a higher percentage return is generally a little greater for all three $100-a-month investments, when compared with a corresponding one-time $10,000 investment.

(17-8B)   *The Probabilities of Receiving a 16% Return*
                               $100-a-Month Investment

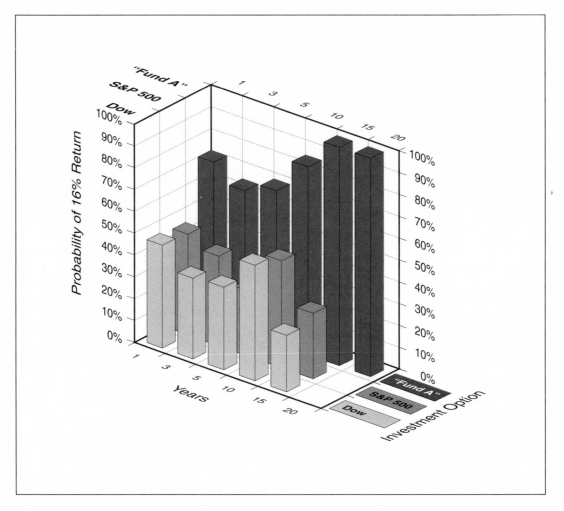

The probability data from the 16% columns in Table 17-8A, under Fund A, the Dow and the S&P 500, was used to create the three-dimensional Chart 17-8B shown on the opposite page. This was done to help you visualize how the probabilities of the three investments compare with each other over different periods of time. Note the dramatic differences between a fully-managed fund and unmanaged investments.

Clearly, professional management and a time-tested discipline significantly out-performed the unmanaged investments.

Professional investment management can lead to real value.

Think twice about borrowing money to invest if you
do not have the means to pay it back at any time.

Borrowing Money to Invest

18

Banks are willing to lend you an umbrella,
but when it starts to rain, they may
ask for the umbrella back.

When you borrow to invest, you use somebody else's money to leverage your opportunity to make a profit. Obviously, when you do this, you must pay interest for the use of the money. While you increase your opportunity for profit by borrowing, you also increase your risk for loss.

Some of the reasons you might borrow to invest:

> For improving your financial position – learning new skills or investing in equipment to improve your future income or security

> For your own business – this investment is under your control and you leverage your capital to increase your profit potential

> For owning securities for long-term growth

> For owning a home which provides shelter, a long-term investment, and possible tax advantages

What is the degree of risk involved when borrowing or not borrowing?

Let us assume you made two $10,000 investments using two strategies:

Strategy A – Not borrowing money

Strategy B – Borrowing money

Let's also assume each strategy could have produced three different results. Your investment:

> Doubled – by 100% (upside opportunity)

> Lost 25% (downside risk)

> Lost 50% (greater downside risk)

Now let's compare the results of the two strategies and their different effects.

Strategy A – Not borrowing money

Upside opportunity:
      Over Time
$10,000 grew to $20,000 . . . . = 100% profit

Two downside risks:
      Over Time
$10,000 fell to $7,500 . . . . =   25% loss
      Over Time
$10,000 fell to $5,000 . . . . =   50% loss

Strategy B – Borrowing money *

You borrowed 75% of $10,000	**$ 7,500**
You personally invested 25%	**2,500**
	$10,000

Upside opportunity:
      Over Time
$10,000 grew to $20,000
   $20,000 minus borrowed $7,500 = $12,500
   $2,500 invested grew to $12,500 . . . . = 400% profit

Two downside risks:
      Over Time
$10,000 fell to $7,500
   $7,500 minus borrowed $7,500 = 0
   $2,500 invested fell to $0 . . . . = 100% loss
      Over Time
$10,000 fell to $5,000
   $5,000 minus borrowed $7,500 = - $2,500
   $2,500 invested fell to - $2,500 . . . . = 200% loss

* The cost of borrowing is not taken into consideration.

You can see that borrowing money to invest can greatly increase your opportunity for profit (400% in this case), but your risk for loss is also potentially magnified (a 200% loss).

If you borrowed the money from a bank and your collateral fell in value, the bank would likely demand more collateral to cover the loan. If you failed to add collateral, part of your investment could be sold and the proceeds used to repay part or all of the loan. If the bank did not receive enough proceeds from the sale of your investment, it would expect you to cover the loss.

If your bank becomes worried about your financial condition, it will likely "call your loan" (force you to pay it back). In other words, banks are willing to lend you an umbrella, but when it starts to rain, they may ask for the umbrella back.

Banks are willing to lend you an umbrella, but when it starts to rain, they may ask for the umbrella back.

Think Twice About Borrowing Money

Previously, I explained how I "traded" $10,000 for shares of Fund A in October 1958 to help start the mutual fund. On December 31, 1991, I could have traded those accumulated shares back into $1,218,215 (but I didn't).

What I haven't told you is that in October 1958, I felt I didn't have enough dollars to comfortably invest the entire $10,000. I invested $2,500 of my own money and borrowed $7,500 from a bank to complete my initial $10,000 investment. In fact, I still owe the bank the original $7,500. I have paid the interest on the loan all these years; but after 33 years, I have not repaid the loan. Frankly, I have chosen not to repay it in order to demonstrate the concept of borrowing to invest over a long period of time.

*In 1958 I faced two different risks: one, the amount borrowed represented a sizable personal risk, and two, the market was **not** at a relative low point when I invested.*

The motive behind my borrowing money was to convince my associates of my strong belief in the future of our fund.

The motive behind my borrowing money to invest in our new fund was **much stronger than profit**. I wanted to convince my associates and future investors of my strong belief in the future of our fund, and in my philosophy which has guided its growth since 1958.

I am **not** advocating the principle of borrowing money to invest, but it's an option you can and no doubt will use (at least for your home). Clearly, you must evaluate the risks and rewards associated with such "leverage." Weigh all factors and risks before making your decision.

**Think twice about borrowing money
if you do not have the means
to *pay it back at any time.***

Becoming Financially Independent

How Do You Achieve Financial Independence?

How Do You Achieve Financial Independence?

19

It isn't so bad to be old OR poor,
but it's a tragedy to be old AND poor.

During your lifetime, you will earn a sizeable fortune. What you do with your earnings determines how much you will accumulate. **Regardless of how much you earn, only what you save is really yours. You can always spend what you save, but you can never save what you spend**.

Consider each of the following questions carefully. The choices you make can determine whether or not you will be on the road to financial independence.

- Can you live within your earned income?
- Have you built an emergency reserve?
- Should you consider borrowing?
- Do you want to achieve financial independence?
- Are you **absolutely** determined to accomplish your financial goals?

Can You Live within Your Earned Income?

The fundamental decision you must make is **whether or not you intend to live within your income**. If you decide to do this, it means you cannot spend more money than you earn. Frankly, this is going to take a **real** commitment on your part. You realize you can't have everything in life. You are forced to make choices. Which of your wants do you desire the most?

The fundamental decision you must make is whether or not you intend to live within your income.

**If you want something badly enough,
isn't it worth doing without something else now,
so you can acquire what you really want later?**

Living on One Income

At the time of our marriage, both my wife, Virginia, and I worked. She was a registered nurse training to become an anesthetist; I was beginning my career in the investment business.

*We both had a strong desire to raise a family, and we were worried about the consequences of getting accustomed to a lifestyle dependent on two incomes. We felt that if my wife had to reduce her work schedule, we might have trouble adjusting to that smaller income. Because of this possibility, **we decided we would live on only my earnings**, while saving and investing all of my wife's salary.*

This decision proved to be the right one for us as each of our four children came into our lives. We were not subjected to the emotional shock of being forced to drastically reduce our standard of living.

Have you built an emergency reserve?

Have You Built an Emergency Reserve?

As I have stated before, having an emergency reserve is prudent. How big should your emergency reserve be? Again, the customary **recommendation** is that you have three to six months of living costs in a "safe" bank account or fixed income investment. You may be in a unique situation where you wish to have more than six months' worth of emergency reserve so that you can sleep more easily at night. In my opinion, however, having a large reserve would not be wise. Can anyone afford, over time, to keep an excessive amount of money tied to the shrinking value of a dollar? I have always felt that I couldn't. I doubt you can, either.

Our Emergency Reserve

*During the early years of our marriage, we felt we could not afford to have a large fixed income emergency reserve. We believed we could not have so much money tied to the value of a dollar. We decided that about one month's living costs in reserve would be enough in our bank account. The rest of the assets were invested for the long term in mutual funds for our future financial security. We actually considered our long-term investments as part of the emergency reserve; that is, we could use them as col-lateral for a short-term loan – if the need arose. In fact, we needed to do that several times. **But we always had the means to pay back the loan at any time.***

Should You Consider Borrowing?

Try to develop a personal strategy about borrowing. It is an important financial decision that may involve a great deal of money.

Our Belief About Borrowing

*When my wife and I were first married, we agreed we would **never borrow money** except to buy a home or to leverage our investments. We never borrowed money even to buy a car. We never borrowed money to buy anything else that would commit us to spending our future income. We have never used credit cards to borrow money. We do use them, of course, but only as a conven-ience. As I mentioned earlier, if we wanted something badly enough, we saved until we had enough money to pay cash for it. But it wasn't as though we were not tempted.*

For example, in 1955, when a friend had borrowed money to buy a new car, we were still driving our 1949 Mercury convertible. Even though we kept the car in excellent condition, it was getting older and looked dated. We thought many times about selling some of our investments to buy a new car. But our desire to be financially independent was much stronger than our desire to keep up with others. We felt satisfied with our decision when we thought about the enormous loss in value our friend took in depreciation at the end of the year when new models were introduced. Our car lost only a little value but kept chugging along. We stayed on track toward our goal of becoming financially independent.

Some people… will receive an unexpected windfall.

Do You Want to Achieve Financial Independence?

When you retire, will your relatives and friends be interested in knowing what kind of car you drove, in what kind of house you lived, who tailored your clothes, or to what clubs you belonged? Or, will they be interested in knowing that you can afford to live in comfort for the rest of your life?

You must decide what you want most. If you are determined to become financially independent, it is really quite simple:

Spend less than you earn, or make more than you spend, and wisely invest the difference.

Are You Absolutely Determined to Accomplish Your Financial Goals?

Some people will inherit a sizable sum of money; some will receive an unexpected windfall. If you are like most people, however, your future will depend mainly on what **you do** for yourself.

If you decide to spend less than you earn, it should not be done just to save money. It should be done with the goal of becoming financially independent. **After you have determined what you want to do, make a firm commitment to yourself to do it**.

If you decide to save part of what you earn, will you still be able to maintain your current standard of living? Frankly, you may be forced to lower your standard of living slightly in order to accomplish your goals. Are you prepared for this possibility? You can easily find out by re-examining your priorities. It takes a certain amount of money to exist. It takes more for comfort, and it takes much more for luxury.

You cannot accomplish your goal of achieving financial independence by wishing. It takes doing. It takes being committed and being absolutely determined to act.

What Do You Have to Do?

If you have decided that you truly want to achieve financial independence, here are some steps to follow:
- **Pay Yourself First**
- **Invest Wisely**
- **Remember the Value of Time**
- **Fight the Temptation to Spend What You Have Saved**
- **Try to Get Your Money's Worth**
- **Try to Buy Only What You Intend to Use**

Consider every month a loss unless you have saved a portion of your income.

• Pay Yourself First

Invest regularly – dollar by dollar.

Consider every month a loss unless you have saved a portion of your income.

Think of saving and then investing as your most important obligation each month, even ahead of paying your rent or mortgage.

Set aside a definite amount at the beginning of each month. How much should you set aside? A simple rule of thumb is at least 10% of your gross income invested for the long term.

An Important Point to Keep in Mind

...if a dollar loses 6.7% each year for 10 years it will lose half its value.

If a dollar were to lose 6.7% of its value in a year, you cannot offset this loss in value by investing your money at only 6.7%. Mathematically, you must earn 7.18% on your investment just to keep up with a 6.7% annual loss in value of a dollar. As I have said before, if a dollar loses 6.7% each year for 10 years it will lose half its value.

If you are having difficulty saving because of an outstanding or a growing loan balance on your credit cards, it may be necessary for you to literally cut up those cards and pay cash for everything you buy. This is an extreme form of self-discipline, but for some it may take drastic action. Whatever you do, make sure you don't plan to save only what is **left over** at the end of the month. Most likely, there won't be anything left.

At the end of this book, you will find a Personal Survey, which can more specifically help you determine how much money it will take to provide for your future financial security.

◆ Invest Wisely

I have never told anyone what they **should do** with their money. Rather, I try to let people know **what they CAN do**. Ultimately, you must make up your own mind about **what YOU WANT to do.**

It would be wise to have your investments diversified, readily marketable and managed by professionals.

Again, one of the biggest financial risks you may face over the long term is the loss in value of a dollar. As I have said before, you would be wise to plan for the worst probability that a dollar may very likely lose one-half of its value every 10 years. If that occurs, it means that all of your investments will have to at least double in value during that time just to keep pace with the loss in dollar value (again, an average of 7.18%

each year). Wherever you invest your money, it should have an opportunity to keep pace with and even earn more than the erosion in value of a dollar. Can you afford to invest for the long term in anything that **is tied** to a dollar, such as bonds, insurance and certificates of deposit?

◆ Remember the Value of Time

Be patient. When you plant an acorn, you don't expect a sturdy oak in a year or two. It must be nourished and it takes TIME to grow. TIME can be your greatest asset if you start early. If you delay, TIME can be your greatest handicap.

The best time to plant an oak was 20 years ago. The second best time is now.

Today, you have more time remaining than you will ever have again. If you utilize the time you have remaining, you may increase the likelihood of winning the marathon challenge of achieving financial independence. If you get off to an early start, it will take less money to achieve your financial goal, because your money will be at work for you over a longer period. This provides you with a compounding advantage. For

The best time to plant an oak was 20 years ago. The second best time is now.

...would you rather begin at age 20 and make small monthly investments or would you rather wait to age 40 and be forced to invest almost eight times as much each month?

example, to accomplish the same financial goal at age 65, would you rather begin at age 20 and make small monthly investments or would you rather wait to age 40 and be forced to invest almost eight times as much each month? (Refer to Chart 4-3 using 10% rate of return.)

One final point on the importance of time: It also allows you to overcome errors in judgment made along the way.

◆ Fight the Temptation to Spend What You Have Saved

Try to develop the willpower not to touch your long-term investments. Keep in mind that these investments are for your future financial independence. Try to leave them alone. When your initial savings reach a sizeable sum, there is a great temptation to spend some of it. You can usually find some logical reason to justify the spending. Fight it.

Falling to Temptation

While I was in college, I used a motor scooter for transportation. Some of my professors thought it was unbecoming for a future executive to ride around on a motor scooter. Their comments upset me and, besides, I got wet when it rained. Eventually, I convinced myself that I should trade in the motor scooter for a new 1949 Mercury convertible. The additional cash I paid for the car came from redeeming those savings bonds I described earlier. In retrospect, I learned firsthand how easy it is to give in to temptation and justify spending money I had saved. I kept that car for a long time.

I learned firsthand how easy it is to give in to temptation and justify spending money I had saved.

◆ Try to Get Your Money's Worth

If you have a question about how much you should pay for something, just remember that it is worth only what someone else is willing to pay for it. How can you arrive at the correct amount? Take time to determine what you believe you could sell it for if you owned it.

Getting My Money's Worth

In 1957 I was still driving my 1949 Mercury convertible. At that time several people made comments that my car did not reflect the successful image of someone in the investment business.

It was too old. In response, I bought a new "ageless" Volkswagen Beetle. By 1959 people were again making comments such as, "If you are truly successful, why are you driving around in a Bug?" I thought these comments deserved further action, so I looked at a fancy used 1958 Cadillac Fleetwood with all the bells and whistles on it. I was determined not to pay any more for it than I believed I could sell it for. I remember paying the Cadillac dealer $2,500 for a car that someone else had purchased for $8,400 only a year earlier. The reason I was able to pay this little was because the car had a new feature, "airride," which had potential problems. It glided on airbags filled with compressed air instead of normal springs and, as with any new technology, there were some bugs. For example, the air pump kept wearing out, but this potential problem did not discourage me. When I drove that wonderful-riding, long-finned car all comments ceased. I kept that Cadillac for five years, drove it thousands of miles, then sold it outright for the same price I originally paid for it – $2,500.

My uncle used to say, **"Well bought; half sold."**

I say, **"Well built; half sold."**

...I looked at a used 1958 Cadillac with all the bells and whistles on it.

◆ Try to Buy Only What You Intend to Use

If you spend money for something you never use, obviously that money could have been better utilized another way. For example, it could be used as an additional investment toward your financial future.

The Most Expensive Dress My Wife Ever Bought

Several years ago, while we were in Boston, we went shopping at the famous Filene's Basement. My wife found a beautiful designer dress that had been marked down to $70 from over $700. She noticed on the price tag that the dress would be further reduced to $35 the following day – provided it had not been pur-chased by someone else.

*Virginia decided to take a chance and wait one more day. The next day we made a special trip to see if the dress was still there. To our surprise it was still on the rack. She bought the dress for $35, **took it home, but as it turns out she has never worn it.***

Bargains are not really bargains if they are never used.

At this point, you might think you can't afford:
> **To live within your earned income,**
> **To build an emergency reserve,**
> **To avoid borrowing,**
> **To save and invest for your future,**
>> **but**
>
> **if you truly want to become financially independent,**
> **ask yourself this question:**
>> **"Can I afford NOT to do this?"**

If your commitment wavers, remember:
> **It isn't so bad to be old OR poor,**
> **but it is a tragedy to be old AND poor.**

Where Can You Find Money To Invest?

Where Can You Find Money to Invest?

*You can always find extra money to set aside
    if you are determined to do so.*

If, after reading the preceding chapters, you are determined to achieve financial independence, you are probably asking yourself, "How can I set aside money when I can barely make ends meet now?" You probably have the means if you take a closer look.

There are many ways of finding money to set aside:

+ **Making Better Use of Your Time**
+ **Working Even Harder to Do a Better Job**
+ **Getting Your Money's Worth**
+ **Planning for Financial Windfalls**
+ **Trying Other Ways to Find Extra Money**

+ **Making Better Use of Your Time**

Time is money. The efficient use of time can ultimately result in finding money to save. Make a record of exactly how you spend each minute of the day – from the time you get up until the time you go to bed at night. Keep a record for an entire month. At the end of the month, analyze exactly how you spent your time. Determine how much time was spent on each activity. Study the results. Were you satisfied with how you spent your time? Perhaps you could earn more money by simply making better use of your time.

Make a record of exactly how you spend each minute of the day…

193

◆ Working Even Harder to Do a Better Job

Are you convinced that you are making your best effort? Do you feel you are an expert at what you do? Can **anyone else** do your job better? Is there any way you could perform better? Are you proud of what you have done and are able to do? Do you believe you have convinced others that you have done your best?

The greatest test of all is to stand in front of a mirror and ask yourself, "Can I honestly say I have tried my very best?"

◆ Getting Your Money's Worth

The process described below will help you find extra money. It is simple, effective and enlightening.

Keep a daily record of how you spend money. List exactly **what** you spend your money for. Include the cost of **every** item you buy. Be specific, not general. For example, instead of using the general category of food, use more specific categories, such as groceries, lunch, snacks, and restaurants.

Try not to overlook anything you spend money on – even interest payments and investments. Keep your information in one place. At the end of each month, the number of items you have recorded will be quite large. Of course, the items will be disorganized, unrelated and difficult to understand. To make the information meaningful, consolidate the amounts of similar items, then organize them in major categories for your review.

Examine your list. Keep in mind that this is a list of **how much you spent** and **what you spent money** for during the last month. After you have thoroughly studied the list, ask yourself:

- ◆ **Am I getting my money's worth?**
- ◆ **Am I satisfied with the way I am spending my money?**

If your answer to either question is "no," focus your attention on the problem categories. You have the opportunity now to change your habits and control your use of money.

This should not be a one-time exercise. Rather, it is a process worth following in the coming months. Your goal is to try to continuously refine the way you spend money so that you finally believe you **are** getting your money's worth. The benefits you will receive from this exercise will be directly proportional to the amount of effort and determination you put into it.

I would like to share with you some examples of how my wife and I changed our spending habits in our early years.

The Lasting Razor Blade

One day years ago, after reviewing our expenses for one month, I became dissatisfied with the amount of money I was spending for razor blades. I said to myself, "If I use a razor blade for more than one day, I can lower my costs significantly." I decided to use one blade for several days and invest the savings. Today razor blades for my new razor cost about $5 for five blades. If I were still using one blade a day, my cost would be about $30 a month. Now I use one blade for four days and have reduced my costs to 25 cents a day, a savings of $22.50

The lasting razor blade

a month or $270 a year. Some of my friends claim they can use one blade for two weeks and one of them even for four weeks. How fortunate, but then all beards are not created equal.

The Peanut Butter Sandwich

Years ago, I became aware of how much money I was spending for lunches. Added together, the amount was sizeable. I was also aware that I had been eating too much and gradually gaining weight. And yet, I was not eating what I enjoy most for lunch – a peanut butter sandwich. I decided I would solve three problems at the same time. If I brown-bagged lunch each day, I could:

The peanut butter
sandwich

*Eat what I wanted (a peanut butter
sandwich),*
Eat less and lose weight,
Invest the difference.

*This I did—and still do. If buying
lunch costs $5 a day, the amount for
one week is $25 and, for one month
over $100 or more than $1,200 a year.
By comparison, my peanut butter
sandwich costs only about 50 cents a
day or $130 a year. The rest is saved.*

Street Parking

*Thirty-five years ago, after reviewing our expenses one month,
my wife made a suggestion. "Jim, you're spending $25 a month
to park your car in a garage at work. Why don't you park your
car on the street and save an additional $25 a month?" I reluc-
tantly agreed. I had to walk five blocks out of the way, but she had
found another $300 a year to invest.*

The Fur Coat

*It seems as though you always want something you can't
afford. As newlyweds, our entertainment was walking and window
shopping. One winter day we walked by an exclusive fur store.
We stopped and admired one of the beautiful fur coats. I asked
Virginia if she wanted it. She said she really did, and then added,
"but we can't afford it because it would reduce our investment
savings." We continued on our walk.*

*A year or so later, after we had saved some money, we hap-
pened to walk by the same store again. We stopped to look at the
beautiful coats. I asked if she wanted one of them. This time Virginia didn't answer me right away. Finally, she said, "No, I don't*

want one." I asked why. She said, "If I had one, I would lose the earnings on the money it would take to buy the coat. Also, I would have to pay for insurance and storage. No, I would rather have my money working for me." This small incident taught me an important principle:

> **The process of accumulating money places a different sense of worth on the value of your wants NOW and the value you place on the money you have saved. If LATER you can afford to buy what you desired earlier, you often find that its appeal is gone and you no longer have a desire for it.**

Planning Ahead for Financial Windfalls

It's helpful to plan ahead of time what you intend to do with money that others might give you. Why not plan that any financial windfall you receive outside of your regular current income will be invested to further improve your financial future?

Sticking to Our Decision

As I have stated, my wife and I decided when we were first married that if we were ever given money, we would save and invest it. We agreed we would not spend it, no matter how great the temptation. We intended to live within **our own** earned income.

Thirteen years into our marriage, I was unlucky and had an accident. I was pounding a piece of steel with a hammer when a piece of metal broke off and flew into my eye. I should have been wearing protective goggles but I wasn't, and as a result I lost one of my eyes.

My accident insurance policy paid me $100,000, a large sum of money. There was no question about what we were going to do with the money. My wife and I had decided years earlier that we would invest any windfall money. At that time we had numerous wants, but our biggest want, by far, was financial independence.

This is why I invested the money. That investment alone is now worth well over $1 million. Of course I'd trade it back in a second, if I could, to restore the sight in my eye.

◆ Trying Other Ways to Find Extra Money

If you get a raise:

Consider putting a third of it aside for your future financial independence, rather than using all of it to increase your present standard of living.

Reduce costs for services:

Become a handy person and take care of your own repairs – but use safety goggles and other safety measures.

Share tools and equipment with friends and neighbors.

"Barter" your services by exchanging your time and special talents or skills for services or products.

Reduce costs of purchases and save on energy:

Buy a **good used luxury car** and save on depreciation – it tends to retain its value.

Own one car and participate in ride-sharing.

Purchase high-quality second-hand furniture.

Make your own clothing.

Save money by buying in bulk.

Take advantage of advertised and quantity discounts; buy in bulk.

Plan your errands in advance to minimize driving around town. This also helps to conserve our natural resources.

Eat out less and enjoy your own cooking.

If all else fails, maybe get a second job.

You may think the process of reviewing how money is spent is boring…

Enjoying Our Money's Worth

*You may think the process of reviewing how money is spent is a boring and unproductive exercise. However, my wife and I have found it to be a great help. Our marriage started off in 1954 with a five-year-old car, a one-bedroom apartment, $1,000, loads of love, and the determination that we were going to become financially independent. In the ensuing years we have lived within our means after "paying ourselves first." At the same time, I believe that we have done **everything**, and I mean **everything**, that we have **truly wanted** to do. We have chosen what we absolutely wanted, and we believe we have received our money's worth.*

The personal incidents that I have described in the preceding pages reflect a way of life that is not unique. Most people who have the determination to achieve financial independence find ways to save and invest.

We are all different and have different backgrounds and experiences from which we can generate new ways of finding money to save. **You can always find extra money to set aside if you are determined to do so.**

The Role of Social Security

The Role of Social Security

You cannot rely solely on Social Security benefits.

As part of your financial future, you've no doubt thought about Social Security. How much money are you likely to receive?

Social Security is a package of protection – for retirement, for survivors and for disability. It is intended to protect you and your family while you work and after you retire. **It is a base you can build on in combination with other insurance and investments**. You cannot rely **solely** on Social Security benefits. If you do, you may be very disappointed in your later years.

Social Security Benefits Can Provide Monthly Income:

- ◆ To you and to eligible members of your family if an illness or injury keeps you from working for a long period of time.
- ◆ For your survivors if you should die.
- ◆ To you and certain members of your family when you retire.

You cannot rely solely on Social Security benefits. If you do, you may be very disappointed in your later years.

How It Works

The first time you came into contact with Social Security was probably when you applied for your Social Security number. This number is the key to the protection you earn during your working lifetime.

If you are an employee, your employer deducts your share of the Social Security tax from your wages. Your employer adds a matching amount and sends a report of your wages to the Social Security Administration. The report shows your name, Social Security number, and how much you have earned. If you are self-employed, you pay your own Social Security tax and make your own report. You do this when you file your Federal income tax return.

Your reported wages or self-employment income is entered on your Social Security record. This record is used to figure the amount of benefits payable to you and your family when you retire or become disabled, or to your family if you die.

It is a good idea to check your Social Security record every three years or so to make sure that your earnings have been correctly reported. This is especially important if you change jobs often. You can get a free form to do this by writing to any Social Security office or by calling **1-800-772-1213**.

The amount of your monthly retirement or disability benefits is determined by a rather complicated computation. Generally speaking, the amount of your benefit depends upon your average earnings over a period of years prior to your retirement or disability. Examples of monthly cash payments are set out in Tables 21-1, 21-2 and 21-3.

Health Insurance Under Medicare

Nearly all people age 65 and over are eligible for health insurance under Medicare. This includes some people who do not have enough credit for work covered by Social Security to qualify for monthly cash benefits upon their retirement. There are two parts to Medicare: hospital insurance and, for those who choose, medical insurance.

If you are 65 or over and entitled to Social Security, you are automatically eligible for hospital insurance.

(21-1)   *Approximate Monthly Retirement Benefits*
If You Retired at Age 65 and Had Steady Lifetime Earnings

YOUR AGE NOW	YOUR FAMILY	YOUR EARNINGS IN 1989								
		$10,000	$15,000	$20,000	$25,000	$30,000	$35,000	$40,000	$45,000	$48,000 or More[1]
25	Retired worker only	$ 648	$ 830	$ 1,013	$ 1,196	$ 1,296	$ 1,381	$ 1,467	$ 1,553	$ 1,604
	Worker and spouse[2]	972	1,245	1,519	1,794	1,944	2,071	2,200	2,329	2,406
	Final year earnings[3]	13,700	20,550	27,400	34,250	41,100	47,950	54,800	61,650	65,760
	Replacement rate[4]	57%	48%	44%	42%	38%	35%	32%	30%	29%
35	Retired worker only	599	767	935	1,098	1,199	1,289	1,357	1,436	1,484
	Worker and spouse[2]	898	1,150	1,402	1,647	1,798	1,933	2,035	2,154	2,226
	Final year earnings[3]	12,700	19,050	25,400	31,750	38,100	44,450	50,800	57,150	60,960
	Replacement rate[4]	57%	48%	44%	41%	38%	35%	32%	30%	29%
45	Retired worker only	547	700	852	1,006	1,101	1,168	1,234	1,296	1,332
	Worker and spouse[2]	820	1,050	1,278	1,509	1,651	1,752	1,851	1,944	1,998
	Final year earnings[3]	11,700	17,550	23,400	29,250	35,100	40,950	46,800	52,650	56,160
	Replacement rate[4]	56%	48%	44%	41%	38%	34%	32%	30%	28%
55	Retired worker only	496	632	771	906	986	1,027	1,071	1,107	1,126
	Worker and spouse[2]	744	948	1,156	1,359	1,479	1,540	1,606	1,661	1,689
	Final year earnings[3]	10,700	16,050	21,400	26,750	32,100	37,450	42,800	48,150	51,360
	Replacement rate[4]	56%	47%	43%	41%	37%	33%	30%	28%	26%
65	Retired worker only	456	582	708	832	896	925	946	965	975
	Worker and spouse[2]	684	873	1,062	1,248	1,344	1,387	1,419	1,447	1,463
	Final year earnings[3]	10,000	15,000	20,000	25,000	30,000	35,000	40,000	45,000	48,000
	Replacement rate[4]	55%	47%	42%	40%	36%	32%	28%	26%	24%

[1]Earnings equal the Social Security wage base from age 22 through 1989.

[2]Spouse is assumed to be the same age as the worker. Spouse may qualify for a higher retirement benefit based on his or her own work record.

[3]Your earnings in the year before retirement.

[4]Replacement rates are shown for retired worker only.

Source: ICN457500/1-90
Social Security Administration #05-10035

(21-2)   *Approximate Monthly Disability Benefits*
                  If You Had Steady Earnings and Became Disabled in 1990
            To use the table, find the age and earnings closest to your age and earnings in 1989

YOUR AGE NOW	YOUR FAMILY	$10,000	$15,000	$20,000	$25,000	$30,000	$35,000	$40,000	$45,000	$48,000 or More[1]
25	Disabled worker only	$463	$591	$719	$848	$932	$992	$1,052	$1,112	$1,149
	Disabled worker, spouse, and child[2]	681	887	1,079	1,272	1,398	1,488	1,578	1,668	1,724
35	Disabled worker only	459	586	712	839	926	986	1,045	1,096	1,122
	Disabled worker, spouse, and child[2]	672	879	1,069	1,258	1,390	1,479	1,568	1,645	1,683
45	Disabled worker only	458	585	711	837	923	969	1,004	1,033	1,048
	Disabled worker, spouse, and child[2]	670	877	1,067	1,256	1,384	1,454	1,506	1,550	1,573
55	Disabled worker only	458	584	710	834	905	937	960	980	990
	Disabled worker, spouse, and child[2]	669	877	1,066	1,251	1,358	1,406	1,440	1,471	1,486
64	Disabled worker only	449	573	697	819	882	910	930	948	957
	Disabled worker, spouse, and child[2]	658	860	1,046	1,228	1,323	1,365	1,395	1,422	1,435

[1]Earnings equal the Social Security wage base from age 22 through 1989.

[2]Equals the maximum family benefit.

NOTE: The accuracy of these estimates depends on the pattern of
your earnings in prior years.

Source: ICN 456000/1-90
Social Security Administration No. 05-10029

within a specified period. Generally speaking, medical insurance will pay 80% of the "reasonable charges" for certain physician's services after the first $50 in each calendar year.

In making your plans for financial independence, you must take into account that benefit levels may be cut for people who retire in the future; and, in some cases, payouts could be eliminated for upper-income retirees. Medical expenses are one more frightening topic to consider as life expectancies lengthen and medical costs continue to soar.

(21-3)   *Approximate Monthly Survivors' Benefits*
                        If You Had Steady Earnings and Died in 1990

YOUR AGE NOW	YOUR FAMILY	YOUR EARNINGS IN 1989								$48,000 or More[1]
		$10,000	$15,000	$20,000	$25,000	$30,000	$35,000	$40,000	$45,000	
25	Spouse and 1 child [2]	$698	$892	$1,086	$1,280	$1,402	$1,494	$1,584	$1,676	$1,736
	Spouse and 2 children*	711	1,063	1,321	1,495	1,636	1,742	1,849	1,955	2,026
	1 child only	349	446	543	640	701	747	792	838	868
	Spouse at age 65[3]	464	594	724	853	934	996	1,056	1,117	1,158
35	Spouse and 1 child [2]	688	878	1,070	1,260	1,390	1,480	1,568	1,658	1,712
	Spouse and 2 children*	695	1,040	1,306	1,476	1,622	1,726	1,830	1,934	1,996
	1 child only	344	439	535	630	695	740	784	829	856
	Spouse at age 65[3]	459	586	713	839	927	986	1,046	1,105	1,141
45	Spouse and 1 child [2]	688	876	1,066	1,256	1,386	1,460	1,514	1,562	1,586
	Spouse and 2 children*	693	1,036	1,303	1,472	1,617	1,703	1,767	1,822	1,849
	1 child only	344	438	533	628	693	730	757	781	793
	Spouse at age 65[3]	459	585	710	838	924	973	1,010	1,041	1,057
55	Spouse and 1 child [2]	686	876	1,066	1,300	1,358	1,406	1,440	1,470	1,486
	Spouse and 2 children*	692	1,035	1,302	1,468	1,584	1,639	1,680	1,715	1,733
	1 child only	343	438	533	625	679	703	720	735	743
	Spouse at age 65[3]	457	585	710	834	905	937	959	980	990
65	Spouse and 1 child [2]	684	872	1,062	1,248	1,344	1,386	1,420	1,448	1,462
	Spouse and 2 children*	692	1,036	1,295	1,461	1,567	1,618	1,656	1,689	1,705
	1 child only	342	436	531	624	672	693	710	724	731
	Spouse at age 65[3]	456	582	708	832	895	924	945	965	975

[1]Earnings equal the Social Security wage base from age 22 through 1989.

[2]Amounts shown also equal the benefits paid to two children, if no parent survives or surviving parent has substantial earnings.

[3]Amounts payable in 1990. Spouses turning 65 in the future would receive higher benefits.

*Maximum family benefit

NOTE: The accuracy of these estimates depends on the pattern of your earnings in prior years.

Source: ICN468540/1-90
Social Security Administration #05-10084

Post-Retirement Strategies

Post-Retirement Strategies

*The dollar will continue to lose value
whether you retire or not.*

When you stop working and your personal earnings cease, there are·
three fundamental financial challenges you must face. You must:

- **Increase Your Emergency Reserve**
- **Determine the Allocation of Your Assets**
- **Decide the Source and Amount of the Money that You Want
Each Month**

◆ Increase Your Emergency Reserve

In Chapter 7, "Planning for Emergencies,"
I described the purpose of establishing an emergency reserve.

Before your personal earnings cease, you need
to consider adjusting your emergency reserve to
an amount equal to six months or more expected
living costs. In addition, you must be prepared to
provide for taxes and unforeseen expenses. In
determining the reserve, you might deduct from
it the expected amount that you will receive from such sources as Social
Security, a pension plan and any insurance annuity.

Most people don't
want to take chances
with their assets as
they near retirement.

◆ Determine the Allocation of Your Assets

Most people don't want to "take chances" with their assets as they
near retirement. They tend to become more financially conservative.
"Conventional wisdom" suggests that people approaching retirement

The dollar will
continue to
lose value...

should shift all or a high percentage of their accumulated assets into fixed income securities. The motivation here is for people to feel secure in the knowledge that their assets are "safe." But can you afford to do this? In other words, **are you sure you will be secure**? Should your main concern be for the **safety of the number of dollars OR the future value of those dollars?**

It is wise to plan for the likelihood that **the dollar will continue to lose value whether you retire or not**. It is my belief the dollar will lose one-half of its value every 10 years. If you agree with me, can you afford to be so conservative that you tie your money to the value of a dollar?

What percentage of your assets should you keep in fixed income securities? The amount depends entirely on you. You must determine how much you can afford to have tied to the dollar over time. If you are attempting to keep a certain percent of your assets in fixed income securities, keep in mind that at retirement you already have a large amount of your assets in those securities – that is, if you are covered by Social

Can you afford to
have more of your
assets tied to the
declining value of
a dollar?

Security, a pension plan or an insurance annuity. Seldom do we think of placing value on the capital necessary to produce a monthly income for life, but this can be done quite simply. For example, if your combined retirement income from such sources totals $1,200 a month, it would take $240,000 invested at 6% to produce that amount.

$1,200 a month x 12 months = $14,400 a year
this figure ÷ .06 (6%) = principal amount of $240,000.

Can you afford to have more of your assets tied to the declining value of a dollar?

The Consequences of Conservative Advice

People who suggest that you shift your assets to "safe" fixed income securities have probably not experienced the consequences of doing so. Take my case as an example. As I mentioned previously, in 1958 I traded $10,000 for shares of "Fund A" to start the mutual fund. Those shares have grown in number by the reinvestment of all the distributions of dividends and capital gains over the years. I could trade these shares back for dollars to reinvest in fixed income securities, but would it be wise for me to do so?

If I did this I would be forced to realize an enormous taxable profit on the transaction. In fact, I would end up owing $261,482 in taxes. Obviously, this tax would reduce the amount I would have available to invest in fixed income funds.

I would end up
owing Uncle Sam
$261,482 in taxes.

(22-1)

Amount Lost in Shifting "Fund A" Shares to Dollars	
Amount received if traded "Fund A" back for dollars	$1,218,215
Less original cost	−10,000
Less reinvestments over the 34 years* from	
Dividends**	− 37,312
Capital Gains	− 423,812
Profit before taxes	$747,091
Taxes Due @ 35% Rate	**$261,482**

How Much Would be Available for Reinvestment?	
Amount received if traded "Fund A" back for dollars	$1,218,215
Less taxes due	−261,482
Less amount to pay off loan	−7,500
Amount available after taxes	$949,233
Percentage lost in this "shift"	**22%**

* Taxes have already been paid.

** In Chapter 15, I discussed the desirability of investing in a mutual fund whose investment objective is growth in value rather than high dividend income. "Fund A" happens to be one of these funds. From this investment *all of the profits* came from growth except for the $37,312 which came from dividends. Do you see why I believe in investing in these types of mutual funds over time?

In this example, my $1,218,215 would immediately shrink by 22% to $949,233. If I took this amount and invested it in a money market fund, what would I receive? The typical average yield was 4.2% on December 31, 1991. This would give me $39,868 a year or $3,322 a month, provided the yield remained constant year after year. But this won't happen. The yield varies day to day, both up and down. For example, one year earlier in 1990 the yield was 7.0%.

*The key point is that if I did this, I would be tying this investment to the value of a dollar. If a dollar loses half its value over the next 10 years, I may have an apparent safety in the numbers of dollars, while I would lose half the value of **my** dollars.*

I expect to live a normal length of life. During that time, I will need money to provide for what my wife and I want in the future. If, over the next 10 years, the value of a dollar falls to 50 cents, how will this affect my family? If I kept the money in a money market fund, I would still have the same $949,233 ten years from now. But, the value of those dollars will be worth only half as much, or $474,617. If the money market fund is still paying me $3,322 a month, I will still be receiving that many dollars, but the value of those dollars will be worth only $1,661. If I did this, I will have "carefully" lost a great deal of value over time. Where will I be able to find the extra dollars I will need to maintain my standard of living?

***If I do not** shift my assets to a fixed income fund, I will still have my shares of Fund A. Again, if the value of the dollar falls to 50 cents at the end of 10 years, where will I be? If Fund A will only keep pace with the loss in value of a dollar, the shares will be worth $2,436,430, not $1,218,215, because in 10 years the dollar would be worth only one-half as much as it was worth 10 years earlier. This is true only if Fund A keeps pace with the shrinking value of a dollar. Would it be wise for me to shift my assets into fixed income dollars? I think not, and I do not intend to do so.*

◆ Decide the Source and Amount of the Money that You Want Each Month

It is a common belief that income can be derived only from so-called **safe investments,** such as money market funds. You need to consider that there are other sources of money to provide for your future monthly wants.

They include:

Social Security

Insurance annuities

Interest from fixed income investments

Dividends from common stocks

Profits from the sale of common stocks

A fixed amount monthly from the sale of equity **mutual fund assets**, that is, a "check-a-month" plan.

Decide the source and amount of the money that you want each month.

Ideal Objectives for Monthly Payments When You Retire

If you believe as strongly as I do that a dollar will significantly lose value over time, what might the ideal objectives be for a personal strategy that will satisfy your desire to receive constant monthly payments from an investment?

You want the investment:

To be free from the shrinking value of a dollar.

To provide a known fixed amount on a certain day each month.

To be adjusted annually for the loss in value of a dollar.

Since there are so many potential sources of income, how do you know which one fits your desired objective best?

The following chart is designed to help you understand the possibilities.

(22-2)   *How Do the Sources of Money Compare With*
                     the Ideal Monthly Payment Objectives?

Sources of Money   **Ideal Monthly Payment Objectives**

	Free from Shrinking Value of a Dollar	Fixed Amount Certain Day Each Month	Adjusted Annually for Loss in Value of a Dollar*
Social Security and Pension Plans	No	Yes	No
Fixed Insurance Annuities	No	Yes	No
Interest from Fixed Income Investments	No	Yes	Unlikely
Dividends from Common Stocks	Yes	Maybe	Unlikely
Profits from the Sale of Common Stocks	Yes	Maybe	Maybe
A Fixed Monthly Amount from Sales of Equity Mutual Fund Assets (Check-A-Month Plan)	Yes	Yes	Yes

* The objective is for the investment to at least double every 10 years.

When you compare the various sources of money described in the chart above, you may identify those that could produce the monthly payments that you want. Only one source will come close to the ideal. It is the last one on the chart, a fixed monthly amount from the sale of equity mutual fund assets. To accomplish your investment objectives, let's assume you have invested prior to your retirement in common stocks of a group of the most successful companies. Although most people have a tendency to be more conservative as they near retirement, I strongly believe **you should consider continuing the same investment strategy after retirement that you were following before.** Remember you may live another 20 to 30 years (or more!) and **the dollar will continue to lose value whether you retire or not**. Why not plan to have your investment last your lifetime and still have some remaining?

A Hypothetical "Check-a-Month" Plan

One of the sources of money in the preceding table is to provide a fixed monthly amount from the sale of equity mutual fund assets. The purpose of this example is to demonstrate the financial results of such a plan.

This plan is based on the historical performance of "Fund A," a fully-managed mutual fund that would produce a fixed monthly amount from the sale of mutual fund shares. The example assumes that you traded $100,000 for shares of Fund A on December 31, 1971. This amount was selected to make it easy for you to understand the results when used in multiples.

Your check arrives by the first of the month. You can count on it.

You initially instruct the fund that you want to receive a $500 check each month for the first year. Thereafter, in an attempt to compensate for the continued loss in value of a dollar, you instruct the fund to increase the amount by 7.18% each year. This rate will keep pace with the shrinking dollar, assuming it will lose one-half of its value every 10 years.

The fund trades back enough shares for dollars on the 20th of each month to provide the amount you wanted, while the balance of your shares continues to be professionally managed. Your check arrives by the first of the month. You can count on it.

Any investment income and capital gains distribution are to be traded for additional shares (the effect of any taxes is not considered).

The following table shows how the amount of your initial $500 monthly check increased each year in an effort to compensate for the loss in the value of a dollar.

(22-3)
Part 1

Check-A-Month Plan in "Fund A" For a Fixed Amount Each Month Increasing 7.18% Each Year

Year End	Amount of Monthly Check	Amount Redeemed for Period	Accumulated Amount Redeemed	Value of Remaining Shares
12-31-71				$ 100,000
12-31-72	$ 500	$ 6,000	$ 6,000	137,603
12-31-73	536	6,431	12,431	101,673
12-31-74	574	6,892	19,323	65,132

But what happened to the value of your remaining shares at the end of each year? The value of your shares was affected by the collective attitudes of people in the marketplace, from extreme optimism to depression. Over the years these attitudes are affected by wars, recessions, inflation, peace, other major events, and optimism about the future. Keep in mind that when the market is at its lowest, you will be deluged by a constant stream of negative and discouraging news. Conversely,

Keep in mind that when the market is at its lowest, you will be deluged by a constant stream of negative and discouraging news.

when the market is at its highest, you are overwhelmed by optimistic news which gives you positive views about the future. In both instances, you must remain aware of what is happening and fight to prevent these emotional reactions from influencing your own rational judgment by focusing on your long-term financial goals.

The value of your remaining shares varied up and down from your initial $100,000 investment and by the end of 1974 amounted to only $65,132 (the stock market was absolutely battered in 1973-1974). Since you did not have a crystal ball, you could not know which way the market might go. If you were **not patient**, if you were **not optimistic** about future opportunities and if you **did not remember** that in the past the stock market, over time, always recovered any losses and continued to go to new highs, you probably would have become discouraged and terminated your investment plan. In doing so, you would have lost 35% on your investment in three years.

On the other hand, if you **had remained patient**, if you **were optimistic** about future opportunities, and if you **had remembered** that in the past the stock market, over time, **always recovered** any losses and continued to go to new highs, you would probably have continued with your plan.

The table at right indicates that the ending value of your remaining shares after 20 years was worth the amazing sum of $2,695,827 (26 times your initial $100,000 investment) **after you received $250,862 in monthly payments**. You may think this is an extraordinary gain, but from the end of 1971 to the end of 1991 the dollar lost 71% of its value at the average rate of 6.0% a year. Therefore, these 1991 dollars would buy only what $781,790 would have bought in 1971, but this is still almost eight times your original investment (100% - 71% = 29% x $2,695,827 = $781,790).

At this point I invite you to draw your own conclusions. Would these results be worth your patience and confidence? **Do you think there would be any possibility of having similar results with a "safe" investment**?

Keep in mind that this hypothetical plan was based on historical results of Fund A over a 20-year period from January 1972, through December 1991. Of course, these results are not necessarily representative of all common stock mutual fund investments. What has happened in

(22-3)   *Check-A-Month Plan in "Fund A" For a Fixed Amount*
Part 2   *Each Month Increasing 7.18% Each Year*

Year End	Amount of Monthly Check	Amount Redeemed for Period	Accumulated Amount Redeemed	Value of Remaining Shares
12-31-71				$ 100,000
12-31-72	$ 500	$ 6,000	$ 6,000	137,603
12-31-73	536	6,431	12,431	101,673
12-31-74	574	6,892	19,323	65,132
12-31-75	616	7,388	26,711	86,203
12-31-76	660	7,918	34,629	131,875
12-31-77	707	8,486	43,115	143,368
12-31-78	758	9,096	52,211	204,144
12-31-79	812	9,748	61,959	347,216
12-31-80	871	10,449	72,408	592,931
12-31-81	933	11,199	83,607	553,601
12-31-82	1,000	12,003	95,610	597,224
12-31-83	1,072	12,865	108,475	737,164
12-31-84	1,149	13,788	122,263	648,400
12-31-85	1,232	14,779	137,042	861,668
12-31-86	1,320	15,839	152,881	1,018,022
12-31-87	1,415	16,977	169,858	1,146,242
12-31-88	1,516	18,196	188,054	1,171,259
12-31-89	1,625	19,502	207,556	1,669,694
12-31-90	1,742	20,903	228,459	1,599,598
12-31-91	1,867	22,403	250,862	2,695,827

the past may be an indication of what **could possibly occur** again in the future, but it is highly unlikely that these results will happen in an identical fashion again. Future results will vary and may be better or worse than those of the past.

Investing requires patience . . .

. . . results don't spring up overnight.

*I would like to be remembered for what I did for others
rather than for what I did for myself.*

JAMES E. STOWERS

I hope my messages have been clear. Obviously, I feel strongly about them. **It is my belief that once you're aware and fully understand what you can do, you don't have to be told by anyone what you should do. You will know what you want to do**.

We all have different wants and place different values on those wants. We also have varying degrees of determination to fulfill those wants. That is part of what makes each of us special.

Knowing what you want to do and doing it are two separate issues. Simply **wanting** is not enough. I have learned over the years that **determination** and **persistence** make the difference.

If you are absolutely determined to become financially independent, you can take the initiative and put these fundamental principles and ideas into use to help you reach your financial goals. To the wise investor, the world is a place full of opportunity where dreams can be realized.

Investing is like planting a tree. Like an acorn, even the smallest investment holds great potential, awaiting only time, nourishment, and the right place to grow.

Investing requires patience. Results don't spring up overnight. Those who look for growth too quickly may cause their sprouts to wither and die, while those who allow time for strong roots to form will almost certainly see their investments mature and flourish.

Because of market cycles, every long-term investment must pass through times that are less favorable to growth. But wise investors will keep their roots firmly planted, waiting patiently for the next growth cycle to come.

As your young investments grow, they can thrive on the attention provided by professional management, while regular investing keeps their growth steady.

When a well-tended investment grows to maturity, patient investors are rewarded, knowing that the strength and stability they sought were well worth the wait.

I recently read an article about finances that included this statement: "**Accumulating enough money is a goal for most of us, but for most it's not attainable**." I strongly disagree. True, most people **will not** accumulate enough money, but I absolutely disagree with the thought that most people **cannot** attain it.

I believe **everyone**, and I repeat **everyone**, **can** become financially independent, **including you**.

If You. . .

are absolutely determined,

have enough time remaining to do so,

invest a minimum of 10% of your
gross income monthly in equity
mutual funds with the investment
objective of long-term appreciation,

and

remain patient and give your
investment time to grow,

You Can . . .

achieve financial independence.

In doing these things, however, chances are that you will have to re-examine and rearrange some of your priorities.

Sadly, it is true that most people will not attain financial independence because the temptation is far too great to spend and live well today rather than to invest in order to become financially independent tomorrow.

Your financial future depends on your desire and determination, on what you want to do, and most importantly on what you actually do.

In closing, I would like to leave you with a final thought. I personally look forward to tomorrow with the firm conviction that it will be better than yesterday – better in every way. I have held this belief all of my adult life.

Share with me my belief that "**The Best Is Yet To Be**."

"The Best Is Yet To Be."

Important Note

This book includes a Personal Survey especially designed to encourage you to think about your financial health, both present and future. This survey can be completed with or without a consideration of your Social Security benefits.

If you choose to include Social Security benefits, you will need an estimate of the benefits that you are likely to receive from Social Security. It is important to complete the enclosed Social Security form, *"Request for Earnings and Benefit Estimate Statement"* as soon as possible and send it to the Social Security Administration. The age at which you plan to retire should be the same in the Social Security Form and the Personal Survey. **It will take approximately six weeks** for the estimated benefit statement to be returned to you; then you can complete your survey. Facts from the survey will help generate a personalized Financial Security Analysis that, in turn, can assist you in planning a strong financial future.

If you prefer not to wait six weeks for your estimate of benefits from the Social Security Administration, you can refer to the charts in Chapter 21.

Personal Survey

Questions You Should Ask Yourself

*It is suggested that you do not answer the questions
directly on these pages. The book is meant to be shared with your
family and friends. Please use the separate copy of this survey
for your records and safekeeping.*

The Purpose of These Questions

These questions can:

♦ Help stimulate your thinking about what you want financially in the future.

♦ Help you determine for yourself exactly what your own financial goals are.

♦ Help you control your own financial future while you still have the time to do so.

This survey will provide a confidential record of your thoughts at a particular point in time. It can be saved and reviewed by you and others in the future. As you go through life, you can complete a new survey and compare it with prior ones to evaluate your progress toward your financial goals.

Thoughts about a Financial Security Analysis

If you would like to know exactly how much money it would take to provide what you want **if you live** or **if you died now**, this detailed information can be calculated and presented in a Financial Security Analysis. Instructions for requesting this analysis are given on the following page.

The analysis you will receive is based on the information you provide from the Survey questions. One unrealistic answer can produce distorted results. For example, when I completed the data for my personal Financial Security Analysis in 1968, I used what I hoped would be a 2% rate of inflation. The inflation rate at the time was about 5%. However, I thought it would decrease in the future so I used the lower rate. Today, I realize this was based on wishful thinking, rather than on reality. So when you estimate what the inflation rate will be over time, use a realistic amount.

You have the opportunity to evaluate two alternatives. The first, **"Bare Minimum Wants,"** should be based on very conservative estimates. The second, **"Ideal Wants,"** should be based on what you would like to have.

The results of this analysis will give you an idea of how much it will take to provide what you want.

If you wish to have your own Financial Security Analysis:

1. Take time to answer the **thought-provoking questions** in the Personal Survey. Some may not apply to you.
2. Transfer to the **Survey Facts Folder** *only* the information from those questions preceded by **a star ★.**
3. Mail the completed folder along with your payment of $20 to cover the cost of this service to:

    Compufacts, Inc.
    P.O. Box 411009
    Kansas City, MO 64141-1009
    Telephone: 816-753-0505

4. Allow at least four to six weeks for your Analysis to be computed and mailed back to you.

However, if you do not wish to request the Financial Security Analysis, you may use your answers to the Survey to evaluate your future wants in broad terms. One way to estimate how much money it will take to provide your financial security is to follow a simple rule of thumb. If you are younger (ages 25-35), pay yourself at least 10% of your gross income. If you're starting later in life, you will need to increase the rate of your savings and investments. This approach is not as objective as the results of a Financial Security Analysis.

General information:

★ 1. Name _____   _____
                                                         Social security number

★ 2. Address _____   ★ 3. Date _____

      _____   Phone _____
      City   *State*   *ZIP*

★ 4. Relevant Information

First Name	Relationship	Birth Date
	You	
	Dependents	

First Name	Relationship	Birth Date

★ Table 1

This survey will be meaningful if the questions are answered from only one person's point of view. **Answer only the questions that apply to you TODAY.**

You may choose three different values for the following question.

A%	B%	C%

★ 5. What percent rate of return do you think you can earn on long-term investments?

★ 6. What do you think the inflation rate will average over the years? ...... _____
      (See second paragraph of introduction.)

★ 7. Are you covered by Social Security? .... _____

PS-5

8. Present Insurance:

LIFE:	Amount of Insurance	Owner	Cash Value	Annual Premium
You				
Dependents				

GENERAL INSURANCE:

Home Owner/Renter .... _____

Auto .... _____

Other Personal Liability .... _____

Other .... _____

TOTAL PREMIUMS: $_____

If you have insurance on the life of your dependents:

Why did you buy insurance?

Are there any other reasons?

If one of your dependents dies, would it cause a severe financial strain?

How old do your dependents have to be before you do not want to protect yourself against their possible death?

9. Do you expect your dependents to go to college?

Do you expect to continue your education?

10. How much would one year of college tuition, room and board cost today for each dependent? .... $_____ $_____
                                                                                    BARE MINIMUM   IDEAL

11. How much do you expect each of your dependents
to contribute to his/her college education per year? . . . . . $ _____ $ _____

BARE MINIMUM   IDEAL

★ 12. You can subtract the answer in question 11 from the answer in question 10 to
determine how much money you need to provide for each dependent's education in **today's dollars.**

BARE MINIMUM Educational Money Required – *Use Today's Cost of Education*

★ Table 2A

Dependents	Preparatory			College			Professional		
	Beginning Year	Amount Per Year	How Many Years	Beginning Year	Amount Per Year	How Many Years	Beginning Year	Amount Per Year	How Many Years

IDEAL Educational Money Required

★ Table 2B

Dependents	Preparatory			College			Professional		
	Beginning Year	Amount Per Year	How Many Years	Beginning Year	Amount Per Year	How Many Years	Beginning Year	Amount Per Year	How Many Years

13. Is there any additional money you want to provide for your dependents?
(Indicate amounts in Tables 3A and 3B, and Tables 5A and 5B.)

If you died now:

14. Do you have a will?

    a. Are you aware of probate costs?

    b. Have you selected a guardian for your dependents?

15. Have you revised your will since your last child was born?

16. Have you established a trust?

    a. Who is the trustee?. . . . . _____

    b. What are the trustee's principal duties?

    c. What fees will the trustee charge?

    d. How much time has the trustee agreed to spend on your dependents' accounts?

    e. If you have not set up a trust, are you aware that a trust might eliminate probate costs?

17. Do your dependents feel comfortable making investment decisions?

18. Who would be responsible for managing your dependents' money?. . . . . _____

19. Whom would you want to control the spending of your dependents' money?. . . . . _____

20. Do your dependents have professions or occupations to make a living, if necessary?

★ 21. Do you expect your spouse to earn more than $15,000 a year? Please answer yes or no. . . . .   YES   NO   YES   NO
(Social Security eligibility question)   *BARE MINIMUM*   *IDEAL*
                                                  (Circle One)   *(Circle One)*

22. Do you want to provide your dependents with the same standard
     of living to which they are now accustomed?

   a. Do you want your dependents to enjoy the advantages of associating
      closely with the same neighbors as they do now?

   b. Do you want your dependents to attend the same schools as they do now?

★ 23. How much do you estimate your final expenses to be?

	BARE MINIMUM	IDEAL
Funeral	$_____	$_____
Medical	_____	_____
Other	_____	_____
★ TOTALS:	$_____	$_____

24. How much would it cost your dependents to live each month if you were to die today?

	BARE MINIMUM	IDEAL
Food	$ _____	$ _____
Rent/Mortgage	_____	_____
Clothing	_____	_____
Utilities	_____	_____
Upkeep on Home	_____	_____
Medical and Dental	_____	_____
Property Taxes	_____	_____
Home Insurance	_____	_____
Medical Insurance	_____	_____
Auto Expenses	_____	_____
Entertainment/Recreation	_____	_____
Other	_____	_____
	_____	_____
	_____	_____
	_____	_____
TOTAL EACH MONTH:	$ _____	$ _____

Other thoughts on your dependents' wants:

PS-10

25. How many months' of living costs do you want to have in your emergency fund?
    (Three to six months, or an amount comfortable to you are suggested.)

★ 26. How much income **in today's dollars** would your spouse need **each month?**
    (Do not include cost of education.) Leave this question blank if you don't
    have a spouse.

	BARE MINIMUM	IDEAL
While your children are in school	$ _____ /Mo.	$ _____ /Mo.
After school until spouse's age 65	$ _____ /Mo.	$ _____ /Mo.
Spouse's age 65 and older	$ _____ /Mo.	$ _____ /Mo.

Use the following information to answer questions 27-29.

   *The dollar figures are to be taken from Form SSA-7004-PC-OP3,
Social Security Request for Coverage and Benefit Estimate Statement.
Approximate figures can be found in Table 21-3 in the book. Or, call
Social Security at 1-800-772-1213 for more precise figures.*
   *Your plans to become financially independent should not rely on
Social Security benefits, but on your ability to accumulate your wealth by
saving and investing wisely. You may choose not to enter your Social
Security benefits.*

★ 27. How much **monthly** income could your spouse
    receive at age 65 from Social Security? .... $ _____ /Mo.

★ 28. How much **monthly** income could each child
    receive from Social Security? .... $ _____ /Mo.

★ 29. What would be the maximum **monthly** amount of family
    benefits from Social Security? .... $ _____ /Mo.

PS-11

*If any amounts from questions 30-34 are for a **lump sum** of money which is wanted at the time of death, include the amounts in question 23.*

*Otherwise, enter the **yearly** amounts from these questions in Tables 3A and 3B. Be sure to indicate **how much money** is wanted, **when it is wanted**, and for **how many years.***

★ 30. Do you want your mortgage to be paid off immediately?
        If so, enter amount in table.

★ 31. How much money is required to pay off other loans?

★ 32. How much money is wanted for gifts to others?

★ 33. How much money is needed for other dependents?

★ 34. Would there be any other requirements for money?

★ **IF YOU DIED NOW – BARE MINIMUM**   **MONEY WANTED** ★ Table 3A

For	Beginning Year	Amount Per Year	How Many Years

★ **IF YOU DIED NOW – IDEAL**   **MONEY WANTED** ★ Table 3B

For	Beginning Year	Amount Per Year	How Many Years

Enter amounts from questions 35 - 40 in Tables 4A and 4B. **Do not include life insurance proceeds in Tables 4A and 4B** *because the analysis will calculate your insurance needs based on your wants and other sources of money.*

★ 35. How much assured income are you confident your dependents would receive in the future other than Social Security?

★ 36. How much income would your dependents receive from your non-liquid assets? *(See liquidity on page PS-22.)*

★ 37. How much would your dependents receive from any pension benefits?

★ 38. How much would your dependents receive from your profit sharing, Keogh plan, 401(k), IRA or other retirement plans?

★ 39. How much financial support could your dependents expect from relatives?

★ 40. How much can you expect from an inheritance?

★ **IF YOU DIED NOW – BARE MINIMUM**   **MONEY AVAILABLE**   ★ Table 4A

Source	Beginning Year	Amount Per Year	How Many Years

★ **IF YOU DIED NOW – IDEAL**   **MONEY AVAILABLE**   ★ Table 4B

Source	Beginning Year	Amount Per Year	How Many Years

41. What would you prefer that your spouse do with your life insurance
    proceeds and investments?

42. What would you prefer that your spouse do with your non-liquid assets?

43. Would you want your spouse to have life insurance?

44. Would you want your spouse to carry life insurance on the lives
    of your dependents?

45. Would you want your family to be protected with health insurance?

46. On whom would you want your spouse to rely for financial advice?

Other thoughts:

If you live:

47. Do you have definite financial goals?

    If so, what are they?

48. What monthly income **in today's dollars** would your dependents
    need each month if you were disabled or out of work? . . . . $ _____

★ 49. At what age do you plan to retire? *(Be sure the age
    is the one you supplied to the Social Security request.)* . . . . _____

50. Could you afford to retire now?

51. At retirement, do you want to maintain the standard of living to which you have
    become accustomed?

52. At retirement, do you want to be able to relax and enjoy life? *(Before you
    answer this question, consider your responses to questions 54-58.)*

53. Will you be as active in retirement as you are now?

54. Do you feel you will be physically able to take care of your home at retirement?

55. At retirement, will your home be too big for you?

56. Can you afford to tie up a great deal of your money in your home when you retire?

57. Will your home be paid for by the time you retire?

58. Where do you want to live when you retire?

    a. Do you want to remain in this climate?

    b. Do you want to live in your current home?

★ 59. If you **retired today,** how much income
would you need each month?. . . . . $ _____ $ _____
                                                                    BARE MINIMUM   *IDEAL*

★ 60. a. What could be your monthly retirement
        benefit from Social Security? . . . .$ _____
        (From data supplied by Social Security Benefit Statement
        or approximate amount from Table 21-1 in the book.)

       b. At what age will you start receiving Social Security benefits? . . . . . . _____
                                                                                  AGE

   61. Do you want to spend all of your assets during retirement, or do you
       want to have some remaining?

★ 62. What is the absolute maximum age
       you believe you can possibly reach? . . . . _____
       (The analysis covers up to age 100.)

★ 63. How much additional money will you need? *(Enter amounts in Tables 5A and 5B.)*

       a. Will you still have mortgage payments? If so, how much each month
          and for how long?

       b. Do you want to pay off any loans or notes other than your mortgage?
          If so, how much and when?

       c. How much money will you need to support any dependent relatives?

       d. Other money for the things you have always wanted to do:

★ 64. Is there any additional money you want to cover such things as a nursing home
       and medical care contingencies? *(Enter amounts in Tables 5A and 5B.)*

★ **IF YOU LIVE – BARE MINIMUM** — MONEY WANTED ★ Table 5A

For	Beginning Year	Amount Per Year	How Many Years

★ **IF YOU LIVE – IDEAL** — MONEY WANTED ★ Table 5B

For	Beginning Year	Amount Per Year	How Many Years

★ 65. How much assured income will you have at retirement, other than Social
      Security? For how many years can it be assured?
      (Enter amounts in Tables 6A and 6B.)

      a. How much will you receive from profit sharing, Keogh plan, 401(k),
         IRA or other retirement plans?

      b. How much will you receive from your pension plan? For how many years
         will the pension be paid?

★ 66. How much assured income will you receive from your non-liquid assets?
      See Personal Financial Statement in back of this book. *(Enter amounts in Tables
      6A and 6B.)*

★ IF YOU LIVE – BARE MINIMUM	MONEY AVAILABLE			★ Table 6A
Source	Beginning Year	Amount Per Year	How Many Years	

★ IF YOU LIVE – IDEAL	MONEY AVAILABLE			★ Table 6B
Source	Beginning Year	Amount Per Year	How Many Years	

PS-18

Your current financial plans:

67. What are your present plans to achieve financial independence?

68. What has been your experience with investments?

69. How much are you investing each month?

70. Are you contributing regularly to a qualified retirement plan?

71. Do you participate in any type of salary savings plan?

72. Are you spending too much on life insurance each year?

73. Are you buying securities?

74. Is there any other place where your money is working for you?

75. Do you have a plan to provide yourself and your dependents with income each month if you become disabled for any reason?

Consider the following when completing your financial statement:

Please list your assets* and liabilities** separately. Do not "net" them. For example, if your house is worth $50,000 and is subject to a mortgage of $30,000, list the house under assets at $50,000 and the mortgage under liabilities at $30,000, rather than listing the house at $20,000.

1. List dollar amounts of all assets and liabilities under the appropriate columns.

2. Next, opposite each item, list the dollar amounts under the appropriate **"Liquidity"** columns.

3. In the **"Annual Income"** column, opposite each item, list the total Annual Income from the non-liquid assets. DO NOT list any income from "Cash Equivalent."

4. Subtract your liabilities from your assets to arrive at your **Net Assets** in each column.

5. Transfer the **Annual Income** figures to the appropriate questions regarding **"Income Available – If You Died Now"** and **"Income Available – If You Live."**

Assets – An item of property or value
Liquid Assets – Cash and/or assets easily convertible into cash (cash equivalent)
Non-Liquid Assets – Assets which cannot be easily sold or converted into cash

**Liabilities – Debts*

Items for consideration:

You may not need to use all of the following items in your statement. On the other hand, you may have other items that should be included.

ASSETS:

Cash – Bank Balance

Savings
Bank savings account
Savings and Loan account
Cash values in life insurance policies
Accumulated dividends in life
insurance policies
Profit sharing, 401(k), IRA, etc.

Securities
Bonds
Preferred stocks
Common stocks
Mutual funds

Notes or Money Due

Real Estate (other than home)

Business Property
Equipment
Inventory
Accounts due you

Personal Property
Homes
Furnishings
Automobiles
Jewels and furs
Collections (art, etc.)
Miscellaneous

Intellectual Property
Patents
Trademarks
Copyrights

Miscellaneous

LIABILITIES:

Current Bills Due

Loans and Notes Due
Bank
Insurance company
Automobile
Brokers
Others

Mortgages Due on Home

Mortgages Due on Other Real Property

Current Tax Estimate

Miscellaneous

PS-21

Personal Financial Statement - ASSETS

Description of Assets	Assets			Liquidity		*Annual Income
	You	Spouse	Joint	Cash Equivalent	Non-Liquid Assets	
	$	$	$	$	$	$
TOTAL ASSETS				**		

*From "Non-Liquid Assets" only.

** Only the *cash equivalent* figure is to be transferred to the Survey Facts Folder.

PS-22

Personal Financial Statement - LIABILITIES

Liabilities

Description of Liabilities	You	Spouse	Joint
	$	$	$

TOTAL LIABILITIES

NET ASSETS (Assets Less Liabilities)

PS-23

The following tables further illustrate the power of compounding described in Chapter 3.

A1

How Much Cash Does It Take Monthly to Provide $100 a Month for 35 Years?
(From Age 65 to Age 100)

AGE AT START

(%)	20	30	40	50	60
0	$ 77.78	$100.00	$140.00	$233.33	$700.00
4	15.42	25.34	44.82	93.21	344.60
6	6.81	13.01	26.43	62.29	257.19
8	3.02	6.76	15.94	42.92	198.66
10	1.34	3.56	9.81	30.35	157.97
12	.60	1.89	6.13	21.93	128.69
14	.27	1.02	3.89	16.13	106.96
16	.13	.55	2.49	12.03	90.38
YEARS	45	35	25	15	5

PUT IN MONTHLY to age 65

A2

How Much Cash Does It Take Now to Provide $100 a Month for 35 Years?
(From Age 65 to Age 100)

AGE AT START

(%)	0	10	20	30	40	50	60
0	$42,000.00	$42,000.00	$42,000.00	$42,000.00	$42,000.00	$42,000.00	$42,000.00
4	1,781.84	2,637.55	3,904.22	5,779.20	8,554.63	12,662.95	18,744.25
6	404.83	724.99	1,298.35	2,325.15	4,163.99	7,457.07	13,354.48
8	97.40	210.28	453.98	980.10	2,115.97	4,568.22	9,862.44
10	24.66	63.97	165.92	430.36	1,116.25	2,895.28	7,509.60
12	6.54	20.30	63.05	195.82	608.18	1,888.93	5,866.71
14	1.80	6.69	24.79	91.90	340.70	1,263.05	4,682.41
16	.52	2.28	10.05	44.32	195.49	862.41	3,804.48
YEARS	65	55	45	35	25	15	5

PUT IN AT ONE TIME to Age 65

A3 — *Value of Investing $1.00 Each Month at 10%**

Year	Amount Invested	Account Value	Year	Amount Invested	Account Value
1	12	$ 12.54	36	432	3,751.21
2	24	26.34	37	444	4,138.87
3	36	41.51	38	456	4,565.30
4	48	58.20	39	468	5,034.37
5	60	76.56	40	480	5,550.35
6	72	96.76	41	492	6,117.92
7	84	118.97	42	504	6,742.26
8	96	143.41	43	516	7,429.02
9	108	170.29	44	528	8,184.47
10	120	199.86	45	540	9,015.45
11	132	232.39	46	552	9,929.54
12	144	268.17	47	564	10,935.03
13	156	307.53	48	576	12,041.08
14	168	350.82	49	588	13,257.72
15	180	398.44	50	600	14,596.04
16	192	450.83	51	612	16,068.18
17	204	508.45	52	624	17,687.54
18	216	571.84	53	636	19,468.84
19	228	641.56	54	648	21,428.26
20	240	718.26	55	660	23,583.63
21	252	802.63	56	672	25,954.53
22	264	895.43	57	684	28,562.52
23	276	997.51	58	696	31,431.31
24	288	1,109.80	59	708	34,586.99
25	300	1,233.32	60	720	38,058.23
26	312	1,369.20	61	732	41,876.59
27	324	1,518.66	62	744	46,076.79
28	336	1,683.06	63	756	50,697.01
29	348	1,863.91	64	768	55,779.25
30	360	2,062.84	65	780	61,369.71
31	372	2,281.67			
32	384	2,522.38			
33	396	2,787.15			
34	408	3,078.41			
35	420	3,398.79			

A4 — *Value of Investing $1.00 ONCE at 10%**

Year	Account Value	Year	Account Value
1	$1.10	36	30.91
2	1.21	37	34.00
3	1.33	38	37.40
4	1.46	39	41.14
5	1.61	40	45.26
6	1.77	41	49.79
7	1.95	42	54.76
8	2.14	43	60.24
9	2.36	44	66.26
10	2.59	45	72.89
11	2.85	46	80.18
12	3.14	47	88.20
13	3.45	48	97.02
14	3.80	49	106.72
15	4.18	50	117.39
16	4.59	51	129.13
17	5.05	52	142.04
18	5.56	53	156.25
19	6.12	54	171.87
20	6.73	55	189.06
21	7.40	56	207.97
22	8.14	57	228.76
23	8.95	58	251.64
24	9.85	59	276.80
25	10.83	60	304.48
26	11.92	61	334.93
27	13.11	62	368.42
28	14.42	63	405.27
29	15.86	64	445.79
30	17.45	65	490.37
31	19.19		
32	21.11		
33	23.23		
34	25.55		
35	28.10		

*Compounded Annually

B1

Amount of Investment......... $10,000 One Time
Investment in......... "Fund A"
(*With All Distributions Reinvested*)
Time Period Covered......... 7-1-1971 through 1991
(*Progressing one quarter at a time*)

Length of Investment Period.............1 year
Total Invested.............$10,000
Total Number of Individual
Periods Covered.............79

	$ Value at End of Period	Annual Return	Time Period Covered Starting	Ending
Maximum	$19,055	90.55%	4-1-1980	3-31-1981
High 25% of Results	15,202	52.02%		
Middle 50% of Results (Mid-Value)	12,507	**25.07%**		
Low 25% of Results	9,803	-1.97%		
Minimum	5,175	-48.25%	10-1-1973	9-30-1974

Length of Investment Period.............3 years
Total Invested.............$10,000
Total Number of Individual
Periods Covered.............71

	$ Value at End of Period	Average Annual Return	Time Period Covered Starting	Ending
Maximum	$46,057	66.38%	1-3-1978	12-31-1980
High 25% of Results	23,398	32.76%		
Middle 50% of Results (Mid-Value)	16,542	**18.27%**		
Low 25% of Results	13,397	10.24%		
Minimum	6,805	-12.04%	4-3-1972	3-31-1975

Length of Investment Period.............5 years
Total Invested.............$10,000
Total Number of Individual
Periods Covered.............63

	$ Value at End of Period	Average Annual Return	Time Period Covered Starting	Ending
Maximum	$80,600	51.80%	1-2-1976	12-31-1980
High 25% of Results	39,110	31.36%		
Middle 50% of Results (Mid-Value)	24,978	**20.09%**		
Low 25% of Results	18,316	12.87%		
Minimum	12,194	4.05%	7-3-1972	6-30-1977

Length of Investment Period.............10 years
Total Invested.............$10,000
Total Number of Individual
Periods Covered.............43

	$ Value at End of Period	Average Annual Return	Time Period Covered Starting	Ending
Maximum	$150,990	31.19%	10-1-1974	9-28-1984
High 25% of Results	108,898	26.97%		
Middle 50% of Results (Mid-Value)	88,200	**24.32%**		
Low 25% of Results	54,877	18.56%		
Minimum	28,819	11.16%	1-2-1981	12-31-1990

Not Drawn to Scale.

B2

		$ Value at End of Period	Average Annual Return	Time Period Covered	
				Starting	Ending
Maximum		$414,051	28.16%	10-1-1974	9-28-1989
High 25% of Results		245,676	23.79%		
Middle 50% of Results	Mid-Value	205,992	**22.35%**		
Low 25% of Results		165,137	20.56%		
Minimum		127,335	18.48%	1-1-1973	12-31-1987

Length of Investment Period.............**15 years**
Total Invested.............$10,000
Total Number of Individual Periods Covered.............23

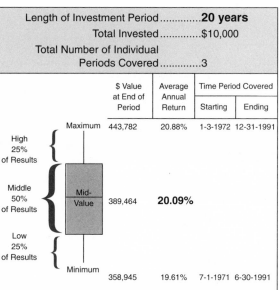

		$ Value at End of Period	Average Annual Return	Time Period Covered	
				Starting	Ending
Maximum		443,782	20.88%	1-3-1972	12-31-1991
High 25% of Results					
Middle 50% of Results	Mid-Value	389,464	**20.09%**		
Low 25% of Results					
Minimum		358,945	19.61%	7-1-1971	6-30-1991

Length of Investment Period.............**20 years**
Total Invested.............$10,000
Total Number of Individual Periods Covered.............3

Not Drawn to Scale.

B3 (17-1)   *$10,000 Investments in "Fund A"*

(With All Dividends Reinvested)

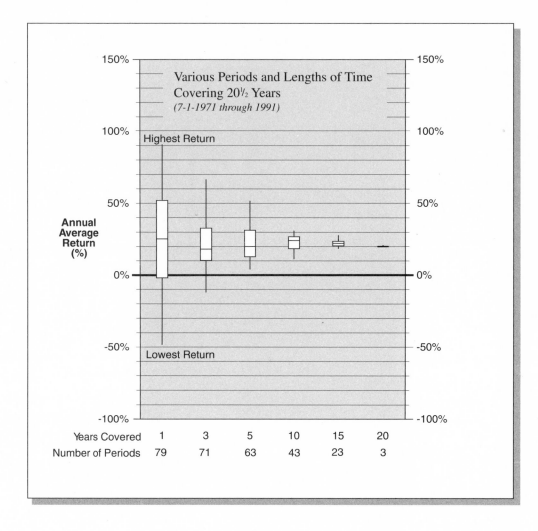

B4

Amount of Investment. . . . . $10,000 One Time
Investment in. . . . . Dow Jones Industrial Average
(With All Distributions Reinvested)
Time Period Covered. . . . . 7-1-1971 through 1991
(Progressing one quarter at a time)

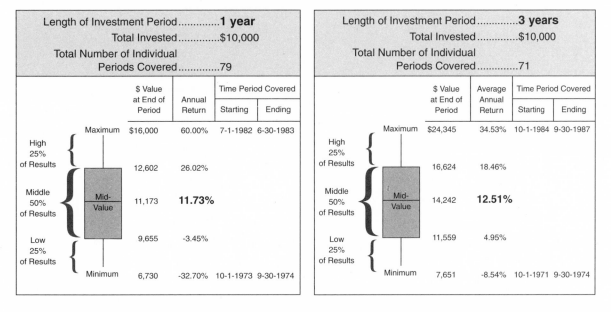

Length of Investment Period..............**1 year**
Total Invested..............$10,000
Total Number of Individual
Periods Covered..............79

		$ Value at End of Period	Annual Return	Time Period Covered	
				Starting	Ending
	Maximum	$16,000	60.00%	7-1-1982	6-30-1983
High 25% of Results		12,602	26.02%		
Middle 50% of Results	Mid-Value	11,173	**11.73%**		
Low 25% of Results		9,655	-3.45%		
	Minimum	6,730	-32.70%	10-1-1973	9-30-1974

Length of Investment Period..............**3 years**
Total Invested..............$10,000
Total Number of Individual
Periods Covered..............71

		$ Value at End of Period	Average Annual Return	Time Period Covered	
				Starting	Ending
	Maximum	$24,345	34.53%	10-1-1984	9-30-1987
High 25% of Results		16,624	18.46%		
Middle 50% of Results	Mid-Value	14,242	**12.51%**		
Low 25% of Results		11,559	4.95%		
	Minimum	7,651	-8.54%	10-1-1971	9-30-1974

Length of Investment Period..............**5 years**
Total Invested..............$10,000
Total Number of Individual
Periods Covered..............63

		$ Value at End of Period	Average Annual Return	Time Period Covered	
				Starting	Ending
	Maximum	$37,547	30.29%	7-1-1982	6-30-1987
High 25% of Results		21,674	16.73%		
Middle 50% of Results	Mid-Value	18,798	**13.45%**		
Low 25% of Results		13,328	5.91%		
	Minimum	10,153	0.30%	1-1-1973	12-30-1977

Length of Investment Period..............**10 years**
Total Invested..............$10,000
Total Number of Individual
Periods Covered..............43

		$ Value at End of Period	Average Annual Return	Time Period Covered	
				Starting	Ending
	Maximum	$54,825	18.55%	4-1-1980	3-30-1990
High 25% of Results		44,706	16.15%		
Middle 50% of Results	Mid-Value	32,796	**12.61%**		
Low 25% of Results		23,763	9.04%		
	Minimum	14,615	3.87%	4-3-1972	3-31-1982

Not Drawn to Scale.

B5

		$ Value at End of Period	Average Annual Return	Time Period Covered	
				Starting	Ending
	Maximum	$92,907	16.02%	10-1-1974	9-29-1989
High 25% of Results		64,390	13.22%		
Middle 50% of Results	Mid-Value	57,175	**12.33%**		
		46,837	10.84%		
Low 25% of Results					
	Minimum	39,464	9.58%	1-1-1973	12-31-1987

Length of Investment Period..............**15 years**
Total Invested..............$10,000
Total Number of Individual Periods Covered..............23

		$ Value at End of Period	Average Annual Return	Time Period Covered	
				Starting	Ending
	Maximum	$89,748	11.60%	1-3-1972	12-31-1991
High 25% of Results					
Middle 50% of Results	Mid-Value	85,115	**11.30%**		
Low 25% of Results					
	Minimum	82,152	11.10%	7-1-1971	6-28-1991

Length of Investment Period..............**20 years**
Total Invested..............$10,000
Total Number of Individual Periods Covered..............3

Not Drawn to Scale.

B6
$10,000 Investments in Dow Jones Industrial Average
(With All Dividends Reinvested)

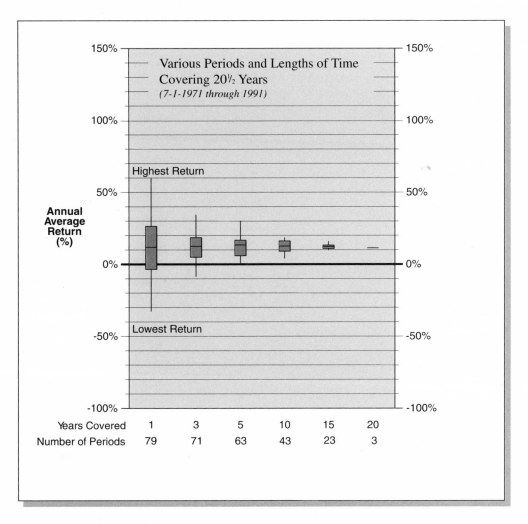

B7   *Amount of Investment........ $10,000 One Time*
                                         Investment in........Standard & Poor's 500
                                         (With All Distributions Reinvested)
                                    Time Period Covered........ 7-1-1971 through 1991
                                         (Progressing one quarter at a time)

Not Drawn to Scale.

B8

	$ Value at End of Period	Average Annual Return	Time Period Covered	
			Starting	Ending
Maximum	$107,134	17.13%	10-1-1974	9-29-1989
	72,356	14.10%		
Mid-Value	61,924	**12.93%**		
	49,265	11.22%		
Minimum	40,491	9.77%	1-2-1973	12-31-1987

Length of Investment Period..............**15 years**
Total Invested..............$10,000
Total Number of Individual Periods Covered..............23

High 25% of Results
Middle 50% of Results
Low 25% of Results

	$ Value at End of Period	Average Annual Return	Time Period Covered	
			Starting	Ending
Maximum	$94,767	11.90%	1-3-1972	12-31-1991
Mid-Value	90,580	**11.65%**		
Minimum	85,921	11.35%	7-1-1971	6-28-1991

Length of Investment Period..............**20 years**
Total Invested..............$10,000
Total Number of Individual Periods Covered..............3

High 25% of Results
Middle 50% of Results
Low 25% of Results

Not Drawn to Scale.

B9

$10,000 Investments in Standard & Poor's 500

(With All Dividends Reinvested)

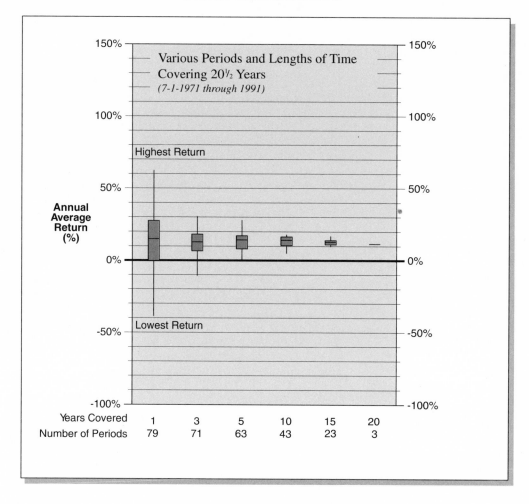

B10

One-Year Results
$10,000 One-Time Investments
(With All Dividends Reinvested)

Results of "Fund A" Compared with
the Results of Dow Jones Industrial Average *and* Standard & Poor's 500

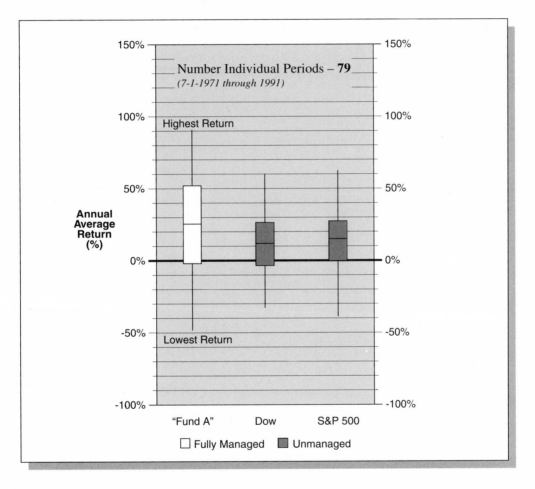

B11

Three-Year Results
$10,000 One-Time Investments
(With All Dividends Reinvested)

Results of "Fund A" Compared with
the Results of Dow Jones Industrial Average *and* Standard & Poor's 500

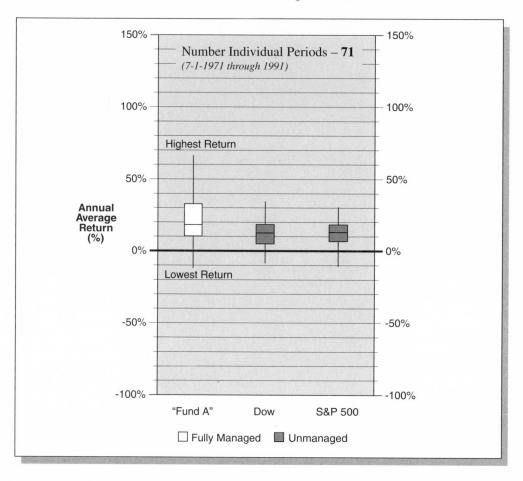

B12

Five-Year Results
$10,000 One-Time Investments
(With All Dividends Reinvested)

Results of "Fund A" Compared with
the Results of Dow Jones Industrial Average *and* Standard & Poor's 500

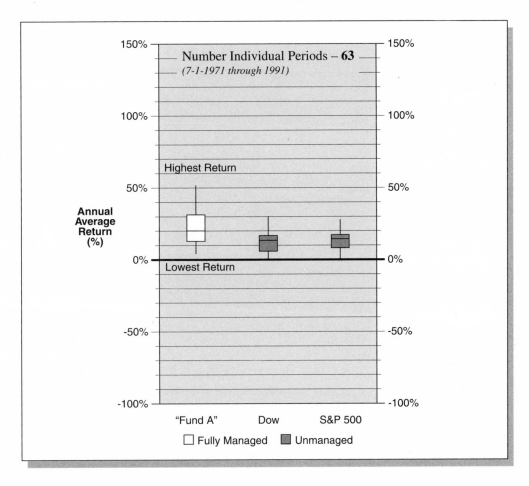

B13   *10-Year Results*
                            $10,000 One-Time Investments
                             (With All Dividends Reinvested)

                          Results of "Fund A" Compared with
              the Results of Dow Jones Industrial Average *and* Standard & Poor's 500

B14

15-Year Results
$10,000 One-Time Investments
(With All Dividends Reinvested)

Results of "Fund A" Compared with
the Results of Dow Jones Industrial Average *and* Standard & Poor's 500

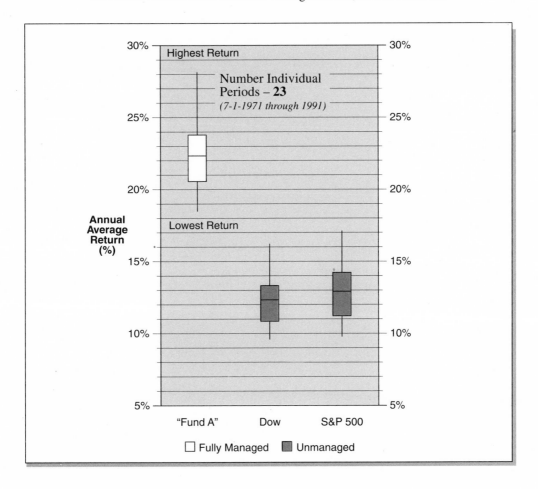

B15 (17-3)

20-Year Results
$10,000 One-Time Investments
(With All Dividends Reinvested)

Results of "Fund A" Compared with
the Results of Dow Jones Industrial Average *and* Standard & Poor's 500

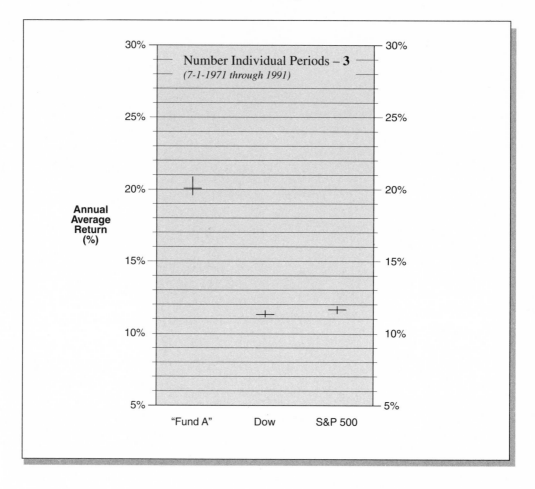

Number Individual Periods – **3**
(7-1-1971 through 1991)

Annual Average Return (%)

"Fund A"   Dow   S&P 500

B16 (17-4A)   *The Probabilities of Receiving a Certain Return*
$10,000 One-Time Investment
(With All Dividends Reinvested)

Comparing "Fund A" results with those of Dow Jones Industrial Average and Standard & Poor's 500

Covering 20½ Years (7-1-1971 through 1991)
*Percentage Results **in Excess of** Various Compound Rates*

PERIOD (YEARS) — **"Fund A"** — **NUMBER OF PERIODS**

	0%	2%	4%	6%	8%	10%	12%	14%	16%	18%	20%	22%	24%	26%	28%	30%	
1	71	71	67	67	67	65	63	61	61	58	57	54	53	49	46	46	79
3	90	89	86	86	82	76	69	66	61	51	49	45	38	35	34	31	71
5	100	100	100	97	94	87	81	71	63	59	51	43	40	37	29	27	63
10	100	100	100	100	100	100	100	98	91	84	67	56	51	35	19	5	43
15	100	100	100	100	100	100	100	100	100	100	87	61	22	9	4	0	23
20	100	100	100	100	100	100	100	100	100	(100)	67	0	0	0	0	0	3

PERIOD (YEARS) — **Dow Jones Industrial Average** — **NUMBER OF PERIODS**

	0%	2%	4%	6%	8%	10%	12%	14%	16%	18%	20%	22%	24%	26%	28%	30%	
1	70	68	65	61	57	54	49	46	43	42	37	34	30	25	24	22	79
3	90	83	79	72	66	58	52	45	38	30	20	7	6	4	4	4	71
5	100	97	83	75	65	62	59	48	32	22	17	10	5	5	5	2	63
10	100	100	95	84	81	70	58	47	26	9	0	0	0	0	0	0	43
15	100	100	100	100	100	91	61	13	4	0	0	0	0	0	0	0	23
20	100	100	100	100	100	(100)	0	0	0	0	0	0	0	0	0	0	3

PERIOD (YEARS) — **Standard & Poor's 500** — **NUMBER OF PERIODS**

	0%	2%	4%	6%	8%	10%	12%	14%	16%	18%	20%	22%	24%	26%	28%	30%	
1	75	70	68	67	62	58	56	53	47	43	34	29	28	25	24	20	79
3	90	87	86	79	70	62	54	48	41	27	14	7	6	6	3	1	71
5	98	95	89	83	76	70	63	57	32	16	10	5	5	5	2	0	63
10	100	100	100	93	84	79	70	53	33	2	0	0	0	0	0	0	43
15	100	100	100	100	100	96	65	30	9	0	0	0	0	0	0	0	23
20	100	100	100	100	100	(100)	0	0	0	0	0	0	0	0	0	0	3

(100) Represents the point at which the highest rate of return occurs for all the 20-year investment periods.

C1

Amount of Investment......... $100 a Month
Investment in......... "Fund A"
(With All Distributions Reinvested)
Time Period Covered......... 7-1-1971 through 1991
(Progressing one quarter at a time)

Length of Investment Period..............1 year
Total Invested..............$1,200
Total Number of Individual Periods Covered..............79

	$ Value at End of Period	Annual Return	Time Period Covered Starting	Ending
Maximum	$1,932	128.70%	10-3-1977	9-29-1978
High 25% of Results	1,588	64.59%		
Middle 50% of Results — Mid-Value	1,452	**40.91%**		
Low 25% of Results	1,273	11.42%		
Minimum	899	-42.69%	10-1-1973	9-30-1974

Length of Investment Period..............3 years
Total Invested..............$3,600
Total Number of Individual Periods Covered..............71

	$ Value at End of Period	Average Annual Return	Time Period Covered Starting	Ending
Maximum	$9,179	71.29%	1-3-1978	12-31-1980
High 25% of Results	5,847	34.15%		
Middle 50% of Results — Mid-Value	5,067	**23.48%**		
Low 25% of Results	4,179	9.92%		
Minimum	2,302	-26.93%	10-1-1971	9-30-1974

Length of Investment Period..............5 years
Total Invested..............$6,000
Total Number of Individual Periods Covered..............63

	$ Value at End of Period	Average Annual Return	Time Period Covered Starting	Ending
Maximum	$22,593	55.89%	1-2-1976	12-31-1980
High 25% of Results	13,517	33.17%		
Middle 50% of Results — Mid-Value	10,004	**20.55%**		
Low 25% of Results	8,740	15.03%		
Minimum	7,348	8.04%	10-1-1980	9-30-1985

Length of Investment Period..............10 years
Total Invested..............$12,000
Total Number of Individual Periods Covered..............43

	$ Value at End of Period	Average Annual Return	Time Period Covered Starting	Ending
Maximum	$75,251	34.48%	7-2-1973	6-30-1983
High 25% of Results	49,365	26.66%		
Middle 50% of Results — Mid-Value	43,346	**24.26%**		
Low 25% of Results	30,042	17.47%		
Minimum	23,067	12.55%	10-1-1980	9-30-1990

Not Drawn to Scale.

C2

	$ Value at End of Period	Average Annual Return	Time Period Covered	
			Starting	Ending
Maximum	$179,577	27.11%	10-2-1972	9-30-1987
High 25% of Results	127,819	23.29%		
Middle 50% of Results (Mid-Value)	122,117	**22.77%**		
Low 25% of Results	111,211	21.72%		
Minimum	89,276	19.23%	1-2-1976	12-31-1990

Length of Investment Period............**15 years**
Total Invested............$18,000
Total Number of Individual Periods Covered............23

	$ Value at End of Period	Average Annual Return	Time Period Covered	
			Starting	Ending
Maximum	$351,911	22.79%	1-3-1972	12-31-1991
High 25% of Results				
Middle 50% of Results (Mid-Value)	299,865	**21.52%**		
Low 25% of Results				
Minimum	217,224	18.96%	7-1-1971	6-30-1991

Length of Investment Period............**20 years**
Total Invested............$24,000
Total Number of Individual Periods Covered............3

Not Drawn to Scale.

C3 (17-5)   *$100-a-Month Investments in "Fund A"*

(With All Dividends Reinvested)

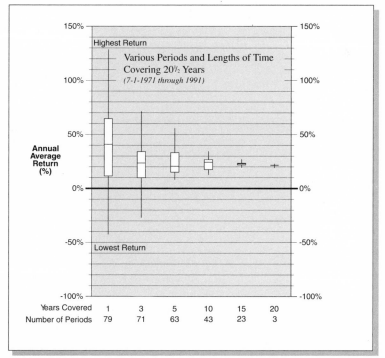

Various Periods and Lengths of Time Covering 20½ Years
(7-1-1971 through 1991)

Highest Return

Lowest Return

Annual Average Return (%)

Years Covered	1	3	5	10	15	20
Number of Periods	79	71	63	43	23	3

C4

Amount of Investment.........$100 a Month
Investment in.........Dow Jones Industrial Average
(With All Distributions Reinvested)
Time Period Covered.........7-1-1971 through 1991
(Progressing one quarter at a time)

Length of Investment Period..............**1 year**					
Total Invested..............$1,200					
Total Number of Individual Periods Covered..............79					

| | | $ Value at End of Period | Annual Return | Time Period Covered | |
				Starting	Ending
	Maximum	$1,608	68.16%	4-1-1985	3-31-1986
High 25% of Results		1,354	24.51%		
Middle 50% of Results	Mid-Value	1,295	**14.93%**		
Low 25% of Results		1,180	-3.06%		
	Minimum	911	-41.14%	10-1-1973	9-30-1974

Length of Investment Period..............**3 years**					
Total Invested..............$3,600					
Total Number of Individual Periods Covered..............71					

| | | $ Value at End of Period | Average Annual Return | Time Period Covered | |
				Starting	Ending
	Maximum	$6,191	38.55%	4-2-1984	3-31-1987
High 25% of Results		4,703	18.13%		
Middle 50% of Results	Mid-Value	4,431	**13.95%**		
Low 25% of Results		3,909	5.42%		
	Minimum	2,630	-19.33%	10-1-1971	9-30-1974

Length of Investment Period..............**5 years**					
Total Invested..............$6,000					
Total Number of Individual Periods Covered..............63					

| | | $ Value at End of Period | Average Annual Return | Time Period Covered | |
				Starting	Ending
	Maximum	$12,664	30.40%	10-1-1982	9-30-1987
High 25% of Results		9,430	18.13%		
Middle 50% of Results	Mid-Value	8,550	**14.13%**		
Low 25% of Results		7,161	7.01%		
	Minimum	6,123	0.80%	4-2-1973	3-31-1978

Length of Investment Period..............**10 years**					
Total Invested..............$12,000					
Total Number of Individual Periods Covered..............43					

| | | $ Value at End of Period | Average Annual Return | Time Period Covered | |
				Starting	Ending
	Maximum	$39,177	22.39%	10-3-1977	9-30-1987
High 25% of Results		30,353	17.66%		
Middle 50% of Results	Mid-Value	28,611	**16.57%**		
Low 25% of Results		21,632	11.34%		
	Minimum	15,272	4.72%	7-3-1972	6-30-1982

Not Drawn to Scale.

C5

Length of Investment Period..............**15 years**				
Total Invested..............$18,000				
Total Number of Individual Periods Covered..............23				

| | $ Value at End of Period | Average Annual Return | Time Period Covered | |
			Starting	Ending
Maximum	$73,406	17.00%	10-2-1972	9-30-1987
High 25% of Results	69,045	16.30%		
Middle 50% of Results (Mid-Value)	63,999	**15.43%**		
Low 25% of Results	57,485	14.20%		
Minimum	52,325	13.11%	10-1-1971	9-30-1986

Length of Investment Period..............**20 years**				
Total Invested..............$24,000				
Total Number of Individual Periods Covered..............3				

| | $ Value at End of Period | Average Annual Return | Time Period Covered | |
			Starting	Ending
Maximum	$119,675	14.16%	1-3-1972	12-31-1991
High 25% of Results				
Middle 50% of Results (Mid-Value)	115,468	**13.87%**		
Low 25% of Results				
Minimum	112,590	13.66%	7-1-1971	6-28-1991

Not Drawn to Scale.

C6   *$100-a-Month Investments in Dow Jones Industrial Average*
                        (With All Dividends Reinvested)

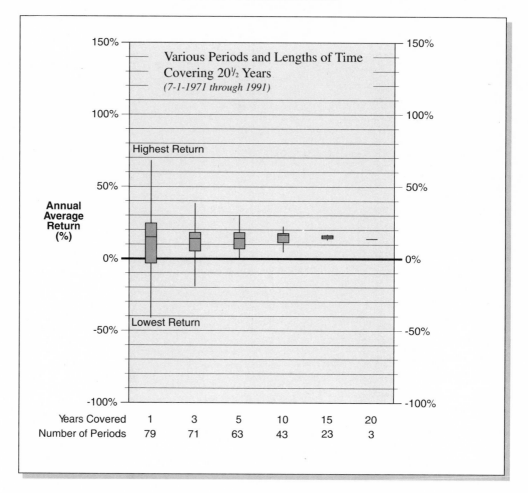

C7

Amount of Investment......... $100 a Month
Investment in......... Standard & Poor's 500
(With All Distributions Reinvested)
Time Period Covered......... 7-1-1971 through 1991
(Progressing one quarter at a time)

Length of Investment Period.............**1 year**				
Total Invested.............$1,200				
Total Number of Individual Periods Covered.............79				

| | $ Value at End of Period | Annual Return | Time Period Covered | |
			Starting	Ending
Maximum	$1,548	57.52%	7-1-1982	6-30-1983
High 25% of Results	1,366	26.49%		
Middle 50% of Results (Mid-Value)	1,289	**13.97%**		
Low 25% of Results	1,205	.77%		
Minimum	860	-47.63%	10-1-1973	9-30-1974

Length of Investment Period.............**3 years**				
Total Invested.............$3,600				
Total Number of Individual Periods Covered.............71				

| | $ Value at End of Period | Average Annual Return | Time Period Covered | |
			Starting	Ending
Maximum	$5,713	32.38%	4-2-1984	3-31-1987
High 25% of Results	4,770	19.14%		
Middle 50% of Results (Mid-Value)	4,425	**13.85%**		
Low 25% of Results	4,069	8.11%		
Minimum	2,400	-24.59%	10-1-1971	9-30-1974

Length of Investment Period.............**5 years**				
Total Invested.............$6,000				
Total Number of Individual Periods Covered.............63				

| | $ Value at End of Period | Average Annual Return | Time Period Covered | |
			Starting	Ending
Maximum	$11,628	26.81%	4-1-1982	3-31-1987
High 25% of Results	9,195	17.09%		
Middle 50% of Results (Mid-Value)	8,632	**14.52%**		
Low 25% of Results	7,588	9.32%		
Minimum	6,509	3.21%	4-2-1973	3-31-1978

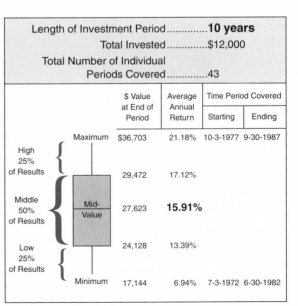

Length of Investment Period.............**10 years**				
Total Invested.............$12,000				
Total Number of Individual Periods Covered.............43				

| | $ Value at End of Period | Average Annual Return | Time Period Covered | |
			Starting	Ending
Maximum	$36,703	21.18%	10-3-1977	9-30-1987
High 25% of Results	29,472	17.12%		
Middle 50% of Results (Mid-Value)	27,623	**15.91%**		
Low 25% of Results	24,128	13.39%		
Minimum	17,144	6.94%	7-3-1972	6-30-1982

Not Drawn to Scale.

C8

Length of Investment Period..............**15 years**					
Total Invested..............$18,000					
Total Number of Individual Periods Covered..............23					

| | $ Value at End of Period | Average Annual Return | Time Period Covered | |
			Starting	Ending
Maximum	$73,147	16.96%	10-2-1972	9-30-1987
High 25% of Results	67,910	16.11%		
Middle 50% of Results — Mid-Value	64,604	**15.54%**		
Low 25% of Results	59,387	14.57%		
Minimum	55,169	13.72%	10-1-1971	9-30-1986

Length of Investment Period..............**20 years**					
Total Invested..............$24,000					
Total Number of Individual Periods Covered..............3					

| | $ Value at End of Period | Average Annual Return | Time Period Covered | |
			Starting	Ending
Maximum	$125,419	14.54%	1-3-1972	12-31-1991
High 25% of Results				
Middle 50% of Results — Mid-Value	118,295	**14.07%**		
Low 25% of Results				
Minimum	114,624	13.81%	7-1-1971	6-28-1991

Not Drawn to Scale.

C9   *$100-a-Month Investments in Standard & Poor's 500*

                            (With All Dividends Reinvested)

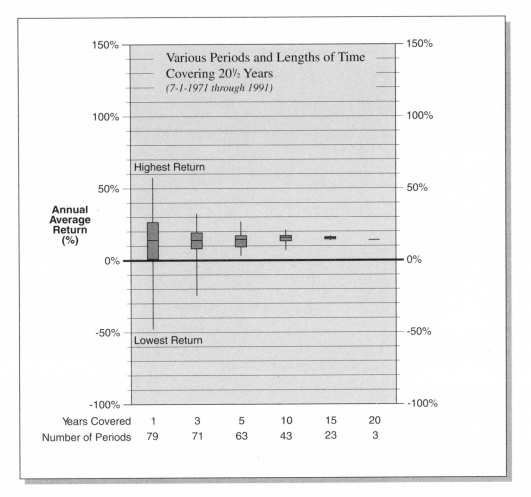

C10

One-Year Results
$100 a Month
(With All Dividends Reinvested)

Results of "Fund A" Compared with
the Results of Dow Jones Industrial Average *and* Standard & Poor's 500

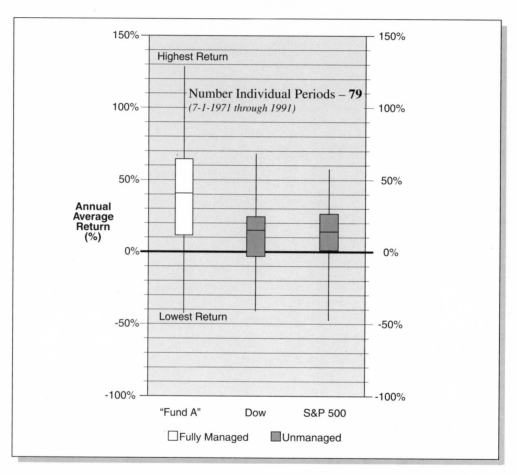

C11

Three-Year Results
$100 a Month
(With All Dividends Reinvested)

Results of "Fund A" Compared with
the Results of Dow Jones Industrial Average *and* Standard & Poor's 500

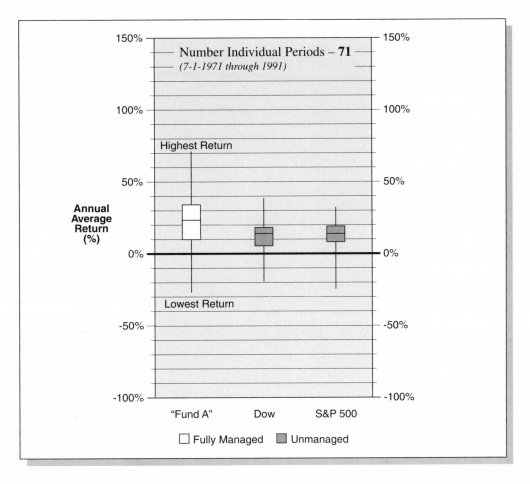

C12

Five-Year Results
$100 a Month
(With All Dividends Reinvested)

Results of "Fund A" Compared with
the Results of Dow Jones Industrial Average *and* Standard & Poor's 500

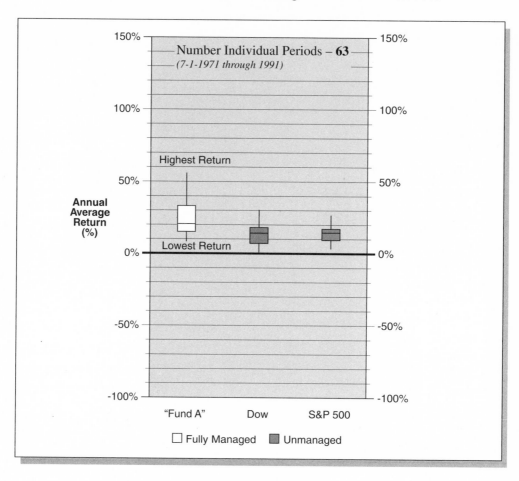

C13

10-Year Results
$100 a Month
(With All Dividends Reinvested)

Results of "Fund A" Compared with
the Results of Dow Jones Industrial Average *and* Standard & Poor's 500

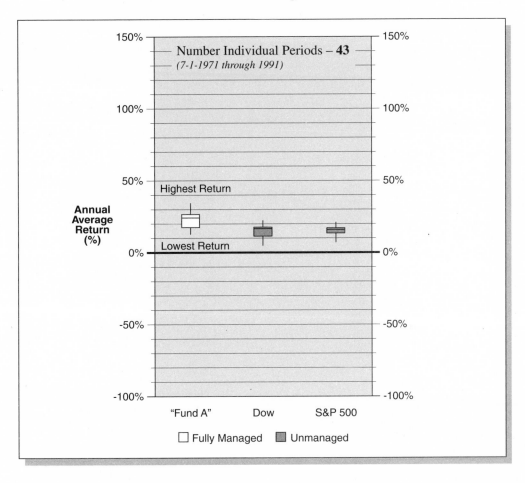

C14
15-Year Results
$100 a Month
(With All Dividends Reinvested)

Results of "Fund A" Compared with
the Results of Dow Jones Industrial Average *and* Standard & Poor's 500

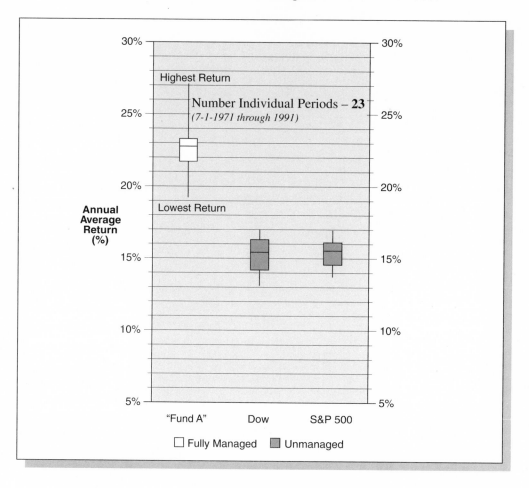

C15(17-7)   *20-Year Results*
                                        $100 a Month
                              (With All Dividends Reinvested)

                           Results of "Fund A" Compared with
                the Results of Dow Jones Industrial Average *and* Standard & Poor's 500

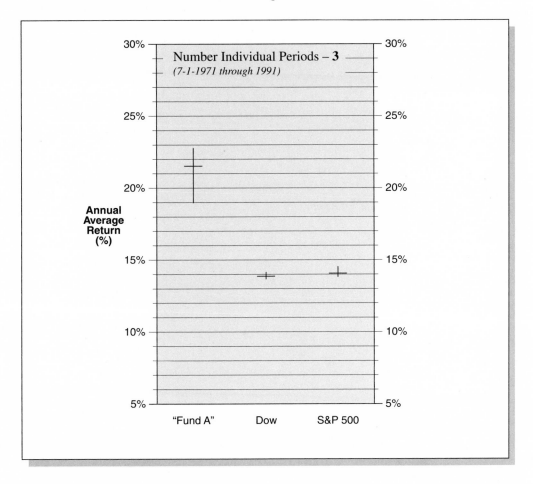

ADDENDUM CHARTS

Paul Coker Jr.
Illustrator

Paul Coker Jr. is a freelance cartoonist from Lawrence, Kansas. His drawings appear regularly in
MAD Magazine and on Hallmark greeting cards. He has also developed characters for Rankin/Bass
television productions, including "Frosty the Snowman." Coker hopes reading this book will make him
financially independent. Meanwhile, he keeps working.

Rick Cusick
Book Designer

Rick Cusick is a well-known book designer and calligrapher whose work has appeared in
numerous exhibitions and publications both in the United States and abroad. He formerly taught Typography and Editorial
& Publication Design at the University of Kansas. Cusick is currently at work assembling an exhibition focusing on his work
in the book arts. His 1987 one-man exhibition of lettering and typography appeared at the Appleman Gallery in London.

Created on a Macintosh IIci using Quark Xpress™ 3.1, Aldus Freehand® 3.1
and DeltaGraph® Professional by DeltaPoint, Inc. Composed in Frutiger and Times New Roman.
Printed and bound by Ringier America on Halopaque 70# Recycled Paper, made by
Cross Pointe Paper Corporation, a Pentair Company.

★ 5. What percent rate of return do you think you can earn on long-term investments?

★ 6. What do you think the inflation rate will average over the years?................ _____

★ 7. Are you covered by Social Security?... _____

★ 12. Answer to question 12 entered here.

BARE MINIMUM Educational Money Required – *Use Today's Cost of Education*

★ ★ Table 2A

Dependents	Preparatory			College			Professional		
	Beginning Year	Amount Per Year	How Many Years	Beginning Year	Amount Per Year	How Many Years	Beginning Year	Amount Per Year	How Many Years

IDEAL Educational Money Required

★ ★ Table 2B

Dependents	Preparatory			College			Professional		
	Beginning Year	Amount Per Year	How Many Years	Beginning Year	Amount Per Year	How Many Years	Beginning Year	Amount Per Year	How Many Years

If you died now:

★ 21. Do you expect your spouse to earn more than $15,000 a year? Please answer yes or no (*Social Security eligibility question*)........

YES NO   YES NO
BARE MINIMUM   IDEAL

★ 23. How much do you estimate your final expenses to be? .... TOTALS: $_____ $_____

BARE MINIMUM   IDEAL

★ 26. How much income **in today's dollars** would your spouse need **each month**?

BARE MINIMUM   IDEAL

While your children are in school .... $_____ /Mo. $_____ /Mo.

After school until spouse's age 65 .... $_____ /Mo. $_____ /Mo.

Spouse's age 65 and older .... $_____ /Mo. $_____ /Mo.

★ 27. How much **monthly** income could your spouse receive at age 65 from Social Security?.................................... $_____ /Mo.

★ 28. How much **monthly** income could each child receive from Social Security? ...... $_____ /Mo.

★ 29. What would be the maximum monthly amount of family benefits from Social Security? $_____ /Mo.

★ Answers to questions 30 through 34 entered here.

★ IF YOU DIED NOW – BARE MINIMUM	MONEY WANTED			★ Table 3A
For	Beginning Year	Amount Per Year	How Many Years	

★ IF YOU DIED NOW – IDEAL	MONEY WANTED			★ Table 3B
For	Beginning Year	Amount Per Year	How Many Years	

★ Answers to questions 35 through 40 entered here.

★ IF YOU DIED NOW – BARE MINIMUM	MONEY AVAILABLE			★ Table 4A
Source	Beginning Year	Amount Per Year	How Many Years	

★ IF YOU DIED NOW – IDEAL	MONEY AVAILABLE			★ Table 4B
Source	Beginning Year	Amount Per Year	How Many Years	

If you live:

★ 49. At what age do you plan to retire? . . . . _____

59. If you **retired today**, how much income would
you need **each month**? . . . . $ _____ /Mo. $ _____ /Mo.

BARE MINIMUM   IDEAL

★ 60. a. What could be your monthly retirement benefit from Social Security? . . . . _____

b. At what age will you start receiving Social Security benefits? . . . . _____
AGE

★ 62. What is the absolute maximum age you believe you can possibly reach? . . . . _____

★ Answers to questions 63 and 64 entered here.

★ | IF YOU LIVE – BARE MINIMUM | | | MONEY WANTED | ★ Table 5A

For	Beginning Year	Amount Per Year	How Many Years

★ | IF YOU LIVE – IDEAL | | | MONEY WANTED | ★ Table 5B

For	Beginning Year	Amount Per Year	How Many Years

★ Answers to questions 65 and 66 entered here.

★ | IF YOU LIVE – BARE MINIMUM | | | MONEY AVAILABLE | ★ Table 6A

Source	Beginning Year	Amount Per Year	How Many Years

★ | IF YOU LIVE – IDEAL | | | MONEY AVAILABLE | ★ Table 6B

Source	Beginning Year	Amount Per Year	How Many Years

★ **From Personal Financial Statement**

★ YOUR CASH EQUIVALENT ASSETS ARE *(from page PS-22 of the Personal Survey)* . . $ _____

Survey Facts Folder for Financial Security Analysis

- Print clearly and transfer accurately the information from your **Personal Survey.**

- Please mail your completed **Survey Facts Folder** with your payment of $20, which includes shipping and handling, and Missouri tax, if applicable.

Method of payment: (Please make checks payable to Compufacts, Inc.)

❏ Check   ❏ Money Order   ❏ MasterCard®   ❏ VISA®

Account number   Expiration date

Cardholder's signature

Cardholder's address if different from address below

- Mail to Compufacts, Inc., P.O. Box 411009, Kansas City, MO 64141-1009.

- You will receive a Confidential Personalized Folder. Included will be a comprehensive **Bare Minimum** and **Ideal Financial Security Analysis** based on the three alternate rates of return and the inflation rate submitted. A detailed explanation, **"How to Interpret the Analysis,"** will also be included.

- Allow up to four to six weeks for delivery.

- **The following numbers and tables correspond to the starred (★) questions and tables in your Personal Survey workbook.**

★ **General Information**

★ 1. Name _____

★   Social Security Number _____

★ 2. Address _____

City   State   ZIP

★ 3. Date _____

Phone _____

Convenient Time to Phone _____

★ 4. Relevant Information   ★ Table 1

First Name	Relationship	Birth Date
	You	
	Spouse	
	Dependents	

Personal Survey

Questions You Should Ask Yourself

This workbook is for your records and safekeeping.

The Purpose of These Questions

These questions can:

- ◆ Help stimulate your thinking about what you want financially in the future.

- ◆ Help you determine for yourself exactly what your own financial goals are.

- ◆ Help you control your own financial future while you still have the time to do so.

This survey will provide a confidential record of your thoughts at a particular point in time. It can be saved and reviewed by you and others in the future. As you go through life, you can complete a new survey and compare it with prior ones to evaluate your progress toward your financial goals.

Thoughts about a Financial Security Analysis

If you would like to know exactly how much money it would take to provide what you want **if you live** or **if you died now**, this detailed information can be calculated and presented in a Financial Security Analysis. Instructions for requesting this analysis are given on the following page.

The analysis you will receive is based on the information you provide from the Survey questions. One unrealistic answer can produce distorted results. For example, when I completed the data for my personal Financial Security Analysis in 1968, I used what I hoped would be a 2% rate of inflation. The inflation rate at the time was about 5%. However, I thought it would decrease in the future so I used the lower rate. Today, I realize this was based on wishful thinking, rather than on reality. So when you estimate what the inflation rate will be over time, use a realistic amount.

You have the opportunity to evaluate two alternatives. The first, **"Bare Minimum Wants,"** should be based on very conservative estimates. The second, **"Ideal Wants,"** should be based on what you would like to have.

The results of this analysis will give you an idea of how much it will take to provide what you want.

If you wish to have your own Financial Security Analysis:

1. Take time to answer the **75 thought-provoking questions** in the Personal Survey. Some may not apply to you.
2. For an estimate of your Social Security benefits, use Table 21-1 on page 203 in the book. For more precise figures, fill out and mail the Social Security Form bound in this workbook.
3. Transfer to the **Survey Facts Folder** *only* the information from the 33 questions preceded by **a star ★.**
4. Mail the completed folder along with your payment of $20 plus shipping and handling to cover the cost of this service to:
   Compufacts, Inc.
   P.O. Box 411009
   Kansas City, MO 64141-1009
   Telephone: 816-753-0505
5. Allow at least four to six weeks for your Analysis to be computed and mailed back to you.

However, if you do not wish to request the Financial Security Analysis, you may use your answers to the Survey to evaluate your future wants in broad terms. One way to estimate how much money it will take to provide your financial security is to follow a simple rule of thumb. If you are younger (ages 25-35), pay yourself at least 10% of your gross income. If you're starting later in life, you will need to increase the rate of your savings and investments. This approach is not as objective as the results of a Financial Security Analysis.

General information:

★ 1.   Name _____

Social security number

★ 2.   Address _____   ★ 3.   Date _____

_____   Phone _____

City   *State*   *ZIP*

★ 4.   Relevant Information

★ Table 1

First Name	Relationship	Birth Date
	You	
	Spouse	
	Dependents	

First Name	Relationship	Birth Date

This survey will be meaningful if the questions are answered from only one person's point of view. **Answer only the questions that apply to you TODAY.**

You may choose three different values for the following question.

A%	B%	C%

★ 5.   What percent rate of return do you think you can earn on long-term investments?

★ 6.   What do you think the inflation rate will average over the years? ...... _____
(See second paragraph of introduction.)

★ 7.   Are you covered by Social Security? .... _____

8.   Present Insurance:

LIFE:	Amount of Insurance	Owner	Cash Value	Annual Premium
You				
Dependents				

GENERAL INSURANCE:

Home Owner/Renter . . . . _____

Auto . . . . _____

Other Personal Liability . . . . _____

Other . . . . _____

TOTAL PREMIUMS: $ _____

If you have insurance on the life of your dependents:

Why did you buy insurance?

Are there any other reasons?

If one of your dependents dies, would it cause a severe financial strain?

How old do your dependents have to be before you do not want to protect yourself against their possible death?

9.   Do you expect your dependents to go to college?

Do you expect to continue your education?

10. How much would one year of college tuition, room and board cost today for each dependent? . . . . $ _____ $ _____
                                                                BARE MINIMUM   IDEAL

11. How much do you expect each of your dependents
    to contribute to his/her college education per year? . . . . . $ _____ $ _____

                                                         BARE MINIMUM   *IDEAL*

★ 12. You can subtract the answer in question 11 from the answer in question 10 to
    determine how much money you need to provide for each dependent's educa-
    tion in **today's dollars.**

BARE MINIMUM Educational Money Required – *Use Today's Cost of Education*

★ Table 2A

Dependents	Preparatory			College			Professional		
	Beginning Year	Amount Per Year	How Many Years	Beginning Year	Amount Per Year	How Many Years	Beginning Year	Amount Per Year	How Many Years

IDEAL Educational Money Required

★ Table 2B

Dependents	Preparatory			College			Professional		
	Beginning Year	Amount Per Year	How Many Years	Beginning Year	Amount Per Year	How Many Years	Beginning Year	Amount Per Year	How Many Years

13. Is there any additional money you want to provide for your dependents?
    (Indicate amounts in Tables 3A and 3B, and Tables 5A and 5B.)

If you died now:

14. Do you have a will?

  a. Are you aware of probate costs?

  b. Have you selected a guardian for your dependents?

15. Have you revised your will since your last child was born?

16. Have you established a trust?

  a. Who is the trustee?............... _____

  b. What are the trustee's principal duties?

  c. What fees will the trustee charge?

  d. How much time has the trustee agreed to spend on your dependents' accounts?

  e. If you have not set up a trust, are you aware that a trust might eliminate probate costs?

17. Do your dependents feel comfortable making investment decisions?

18. Who would be responsible for managing your dependents' money?.............. _____

19. Whom would you want to control the spending of your dependents' money?.............. _____

20. Do your dependents have professions or occupations to make a living, if necessary?

★ 21. Do you expect your spouse to earn more than $15,000 a year? Please answer yes or no............... *(Social Security eligibility question)*

YES	NO		YES	NO
BARE MINIMUM (Circle One)			*IDEAL* (Circle One)	

22. Do you want to provide your dependents with the same standard
    of living to which they are now accustomed?

    a. Do you want your dependents to live in the same or a similiar neighborhood
        as they do now?

    b. Do you want your dependents to attend the same schools as they do now?

★ 23. How much do you estimate your final expenses to be?

	BARE MINIMUM	IDEAL
Funeral	$ _____	$ _____
Medical	_____	_____
Other	_____	_____
★ TOTALS:	$ _____	$ _____

24. How much would it cost your dependents to live each month if you were
to die today?

	BARE MINIMUM	IDEAL
Food	$ _____	$ _____
Rent/Mortgage	_____	_____
Clothing	_____	_____
Utilities	_____	_____
Upkeep on Home	_____	_____
Medical and Dental	_____	_____
Property Taxes	_____	_____
Home Insurance	_____	_____
Medical Insurance	_____	_____
Auto Expenses	_____	_____
Entertainment/Recreation	_____	_____
Other	_____	_____
	_____	_____
	_____	_____
	_____	_____
	_____	_____
TOTAL EACH MONTH:	$ _____	$ _____

Other thoughts on your dependents' wants:

25. How many months' of living costs do you want to have in your emergency fund?
    (Three to six months, or an amount comfortable to you are suggested.)

★ 26. How much income **in today's dollars** would your spouse need **each month?**
    (Do not include cost of education.) Leave this question blank if you don't
    have a spouse.

	BARE MINIMUM	IDEAL
While your children are in school	$_____ /Mo.	$_____ /Mo.
After school until spouse's age 65	$_____ /Mo.	$_____ /Mo.
Spouse's age 65 and older	$_____ /Mo.	$_____ /Mo.

Use the following information to answer questions 27- 29.

*For an estimate of your Social Security benefits, use Table 21-1
on page 203 in the book. For more precise figures, fill out and mail the
Social Sercurity Form bound in this workbook.*
*Your plans to become financially independent should not rely on
Social Security benefits, but on your ability to accumulate your wealth by
saving and investing wisely. You may choose not to enter your Social
Security benefits.*

★ 27. How much **monthly** income could your spouse
    receive at age 65 from Social Security?.............................. $_____ /Mo.

★ 28. How much **monthly** income could each child
    receive from Social Security?.. $_____ /Mo.

★ 29. What would be the maximum **monthly** amount of family
    benefits from Social Security?.. $_____ /Mo.

*If any amounts from questions 30-34 are for a **lump sum** of money which is wanted at the time of death, include the amounts in question 23.*

*Otherwise, enter the **yearly** amounts from these questions in Tables 3A and 3B. Be sure to indicate **how much money** is wanted, **when it is wanted,** and for **how many years.***

★ 30. Do you want your mortgage to be paid off immediately?
       If so, enter amount in table.

★ 31. How much money is required to pay off other loans?

★ 32. How much money is wanted for gifts to others?

★ 33. How much money is needed for other dependents?

★ 34. Would there be any other requirements for money?

★ IF YOU DIED NOW – BARE MINIMUM	MONEY WANTED			★ Table 3A
For	*Beginning Year*	*Amount Per Year*	*How Many Years*	

★ IF YOU DIED NOW – IDEAL	MONEY WANTED			★ Table 3B
For	*Beginning Year*	*Amount Per Year*	*How Many Years*	

SOCIAL SECURITY ADMINISTRATION

Request for Earnings and Benefit Estimate Statement

The Social Security program belongs to you and you can count on it to be there for you. Social Security can protect you in many ways. It can help support your family in the event of your death and provide monthly payments and health insurance when you retire or if you become disabled.

To help you learn how Social Security is a part of your life, we are pleased to offer you a free Personal Earnings and Benefit Estimate Statement.

The Personal Earnings and Benefit Estimate Statement shows your Social Security earnings history and estimates how much you have paid in Social Security taxes. It also estimates your future benefits and tells you how you can qualify for benefits. When you receive your earnings statement, we hope you will use it to start planning for a strong financial future.

To receive your statement, please fill out the form on the reverse and mail it to us. You should receive your statement in 6 weeks or less. We look forward to sending it to you.

GWENDOLYN S. KING
Commissioner of Social Security

SOCIAL SECURITY ADMINISTRATION
Request for Earnings and Benefit Estimat

To receive a free statement of your earnings covered by Social Security and your estimated future benefits, all you need to do is fill out this form Please print or type your answers. When you have completed the form, fold it and mail it to us.

1. Name shown on your Social Security card:

   _____   _____   _____
   First   Middle Initial   Last

2. Your Social Security number as shown on your card:

   ☐ ☐ ☐ – ☐ ☐ – ☐ ☐ ☐ ☐

3. Your date of birth: _____   _____   _____
                        Month   Day   Year

4. Other Social Security numbers you have used:

   ☐ ☐ ☐ – ☐ ☐ – ☐ ☐ ☐ ☐

   ☐ ☐ ☐ – ☐ ☐ – ☐ ☐ ☐ ☐

5. Your Sex: ☐ Male   ☐ Female

6. Other names you have used (including a maiden name):

   _____

   _____

7. Show your actual earnings for last year and your estimated earnings for this year. Include only wages and/or net self-employment income covered by Social Security.

   A. Last year's actual earnings:

      $ ☐ ☐ ☐ , ☐ ☐ ☐ . 0 0
        Dollars only

   B. This year's estimated earnings:

      $ ☐ ☐ ☐ , ☐ ☐ ☐ . 0 0
        Dollars only

8. Show the age at which you plan to retire: ☐ ☐

                                               (Show only one age)

Form Approved
OMB No. 0960-0466

SP

tatement

9. Below, show the average yearly amount that you think you will earn **between now and when you plan to retire.** Your estimate of future earnings will be added to those earnings already on our records to give you the best possible estimate.

   Enter a yearly average, not your total future lifetime earnings. Only show earnings covered by Social Security. Do not add cost-of-living, performance or scheduled pay increases or bonuses. The reason for this is that we estimate retirement benefits in today's dollars, but adjust them to account for average wage growth in the national economy.

   However, if you expect to earn significantly more or less in the future due to promotions, job changes, part-time work, or an absence from the work force, enter the amount in today's dollars that most closely reflects your future average yearly earnings.

   Most people should enter the same amount that they are earning now (the amount shown in 7B).

   Your future average yearly earnings:

   $ Dollars only .0 0

10. Address where you want us to send the statement:

   Name

   Street Address (Include Apt. No., P.O. Box, or Rural Route)

   City   State   Zip Code

   I am asking for information about my own Social Security record or the record of a person I am authorized to represent. I understand that if I deliberately request information under false pretenses I may be guilty of a federal crime and could be fined and/or imprisoned. I authorize you to send the statement of earnings and benefit estimates to the person named in item 10 through a contractor.

   Please sign your name (Do not print)

   Date   (Area Code) Daytime Telephone No.

We estimate that it will take you about 5 minutes to complete this form. This includes the time it will take to read the instructions, gather the necessary facts and fill out the form. If you have comments or suggestions on this estimate, or on any other aspect of this form, write to the Social Security Administration, ATTN: Reports Clearance Officer, 1-A-21 Operations Bldg., Baltimore, MD 21235, and to the Office of Management and Budget, Paperwork Reduction Project (0960-0466), Washington, D.C. 20503. **Do not send completed forms or information concerning your claim to these offices. Send them to your nearest Social Security Office.**

Enter amounts from questions 35-40 in Tables 4A and 4B. **Do not include life insurance proceeds in Tables 4A and 4B** because the analysis will calculate your insurance needs based on your wants and other sources of money.

★ 35. How much assured income are you confident your dependents would receive in the future other than Social Security? *(Do not include: dividends on securities or interest. List income items such as: rental property, insurance annuities, pension plans monthly or lump sum, etc.)*

★ 36. How much income would your dependents receive from your non-liquid assets? *(See liquidity on page PS-22.)*

★ 37. How much would your dependents receive from any pension benefits?

★ 38. How much would your dependents receive from your profit sharing, Keogh plan, 401(k), IRA or other retirement plans?

★ 39. How much financial support could your dependents expect from relatives?

★ 40. How much can you expect from an inheritance?

★ **IF YOU DIED NOW – BARE MINIMUM**   **MONEY AVAILABLE**   ★ Table 4A

Source	Beginning Year	Amount Per Year	How Many Years

★ **IF YOU DIED NOW – IDEAL**   **MONEY AVAILABLE**   ★ Table 4B

Source	Beginning Year	Amount Per Year	How Many Years

41. What would you prefer that your spouse do with your life insurance proceeds and investments?

42. What would you prefer that your spouse do with your non-liquid assets?

43. Would you want your spouse to have life insurance?

44. Would you want your spouse to carry life insurance on the lives of your dependents?

45. Would you want your family to be protected with health insurance?

46. On whom would you want your spouse to rely for financial advice?

Other thoughts:

If you live:

47. Do you have definite financial goals?

    If so, what are they?

48. What monthly income **in today's dollars** would your dependents
    need each month if you were disabled or out of work? . . . . $ _____

★ 49. At what age do you plan to retire? *(Be sure the age
    is the one you supplied to the Social Security request.)* . . . . _____

50. Could you afford to retire now?

51. At retirement, do you want to maintain the standard of living to which you have
    become accustomed?

52. At retirement, do you want to be able to relax and enjoy life? *(Before you
    answer this question, consider your responses to questions 54-58.)*

53. Will you be as active in retirement as you are now?

54. Do you feel you will be physically able to take care of your home at retirement?

55. At retirement, will your home be too big for you?

56. Can you afford to tie up a great deal of your money in your home when you retire?

57. Will your home be paid for by the time you retire?

58. Where do you want to live when you retire?

    a. Do you want to remain in this climate?

    b. Do you want to live in your current home?

★ 59. If you **retired today,** how much income
        would you need **each month?** . . . . $ _____ /Mo. $ _____ /Mo.
                                                                        BARE MINIMUM   IDEAL

★ 60. a. What could be your monthly retirement
           benefit from Social Security? . . . .$ _____
           *(From data supplied by Social Security Benefit Statement
           or approximate amount from Table 21-1 in the book.)*

        b. At what age will you start receiving Social Security benefits? . . . . . . _____
                                                                                        AGE

  61. Do you want to spend all of your assets during retirement, or do you
       want to have some remaining?

★ 62. What is the absolute maximum age
        you believe you can possibly reach? . . . . _____
        (The analysis covers up to age 100.)

★ 63. How much additional money will you need? *(Enter amounts in Tables 5A and 5B.)*

        a. Will you still have mortgage payments? If so, how much each month
            and for how long?

        b. Do you want to pay off any loans or notes other than your mortgage?
            If so, how much and when?

        c. How much money will you need to support any dependent relatives?

        d. Other money for the things you have always wanted to do:

★ 64. Is there any additional money you want to cover such things as a nursing home
        and medical care contingencies? *(Enter amounts in Tables 5A and 5B.)*

★ **IF YOU LIVE – BARE MINIMUM**   **MONEY WANTED**   ★ Table 5A

For	Beginning Year	Amount Per Year	How Many Years

★ **IF YOU LIVE – IDEAL**   **MONEY WANTED**   ★ Table 5B

For	Beginning Year	Amount Per Year	How Many Years

★ 65. How much assured income will you have at retirement, other than Social
     Security? For how many years can it be assured?
     (Enter amounts in Tables 6A and 6B.)

     a. How much will you receive from profit sharing, Keogh plan, 401(k),
        IRA or other retirement plans?

     b. How much will you receive from your pension plan? For how many years
        will the pension be paid?

★ 66. How much assured income will you receive from your non-liquid assets?
     See Personal Financial Statement in back of this book. *(Enter amounts in Tables
     6A and 6B.)*

★

IF YOU LIVE – BARE MINIMUM		MONEY AVAILABLE		★ Table 6A
Source	Beginning Year	Amount Per Year	How Many Years	

★

IF YOU LIVE – IDEAL		MONEY AVAILABLE		★ Table 6B
Source	Beginning Year	Amount Per Year	How Many Years	

Your current financial plans:

67. What are your present plans to achieve financial independence?

68. What has been your experience with investments?

69. How much are you investing each month?

70. Are you contributing regularly to a qualified retirement plan?

71. Do you participate in any type of salary savings plan?

72. Are you spending too much on life insurance each year?

73. Are you buying securities?

74. Is there any other place where your money is working for you?

75. Do you have a plan to provide yourself and your dependents with income each month if you become disabled for any reason?

Consider the following when completing your financial statement:

Please list your assets* and liabilities** separately. Do not "net" them. For example, if your house is worth $50,000 and is subject to a mortgage of $30,000, list the house under assets at $50,000 and the mortgage under liabilities at $30,000, rather than listing the house at $20,000.

1. List dollar amounts of all assets and liabilities under the appropriate columns.

2. Next, opposite each item, list the dollar amounts under the appropriate **"Liquidity"** columns.

3. In the **"Annual Income"** column, opposite each item, list the total Annual Income from the non-liquid assets. DO NOT list any income from "Cash Equivalent."

4. Subtract your liabilities from your assets to arrive at your **Net Assets** in each column.

5. Transfer the **Annual Income** figures to the appropriate questions regarding **"Income Available – If You Died Now"** and **"Income Available – If You Live."**

* *Assets – An item of property or value*
  Liquid Assets – Cash and/or assets easily convertible into cash (cash equivalent)
  Non-Liquid Assets – Assets which cannot be easily sold or converted into cash

** *Liabilities – Debts*

Items for consideration:

You may not need to use all of the following items in your statement. On the other hand, you may have other items that should be included.

ASSETS:

Cash – Bank Balance

Savings
    Bank savings account
    Savings and Loan account
    Cash values in life insurance policies
    Accumulated dividends in life
        insurance policies
    Profit sharing, 401(k), IRA, etc.

Securities
    Bonds
    Preferred stocks
    Common stocks
    Mutual funds

Notes or Money Due

Real Estate (other than home)

Business Property
    Equipment
    Inventory
    Accounts due you

Personal Property
    Homes
    Furnishings
    Automobiles
    Jewels and furs
    Collections (art, etc.)
    Miscellaneous

Intellectual Property
    Patents
    Trademarks
    Copyrights

Miscellaneous

LIABILITIES:

Current Bills Due

Loans and Notes Due
    Bank
    Insurance company
    Automobile
    Brokers
    Others

Mortgages Due on Home

Mortgages Due on Other Real Property

Current Tax Estimate

Miscellaneous

Personal Financial Statement - ASSETS

Description of Assets

Assets

You   Spouse   Joint

Liquidity

Cash Equivalent   Non-Liquid Assets

*Annual Income

TOTAL ASSETS

*From "Non-Liquid Assets" only.

**Only the *cash equivalent* figure is to be transferred to the Survey Facts Folder.*

Personal Financial Statement - LIABILITIES

Description of Liabilities	Liabilities		
	You	Spouse	Joint
	$	$	$

TOTAL LIABILITIES

NET ASSETS (Assets Less Liabilities)

012-COO2